T0197208

Also by

Gregor Collins

*The Accidental Caregiver: How I Met, Loved, and Lost
Legendary Holocaust Refugee Maria Altmann*

The Accidental Caregiver

PART II

Saying YES to a World without Maria Altmann

GREGOR COLLINS

BALBOA.PRESS
A DIVISION OF HAY HOUSE

Copyright © 2020 Gregor Collins.

All rights reserved. No part of this book may be used or reproduced by any means, graphic, electronic, or mechanical, including photocopying, recording, taping or by any information storage retrieval system without the written permission of the author except in the case of brief quotations embodied in critical articles and reviews.

Balboa Press books may be ordered through booksellers or by contacting:

Balboa Press
A Division of Hay House
1663 Liberty Drive
Bloomington, IN 47403
www.balboapress.com
844-682-1282

Because of the dynamic nature of the Internet, any web addresses or links contained in this book may have changed since publication and may no longer be valid. The views expressed in this work are solely those of the author and do not necessarily reflect the views of the publisher, and the publisher hereby disclaims any responsibility for them.

The author of this book does not dispense medical advice or prescribe the use of any technique as a form of treatment for physical, emotional, or medical problems without the advice of a physician, either directly or indirectly. The intent of the author is only to offer information of a general nature to help you in your quest for emotional and spiritual well-being. In the event you use any of the information in this book for yourself, which is your constitutional right, the author and the publisher assume no responsibility for your actions.

Any people depicted in stock imagery provided by Getty Images are models, and such images are being used for illustrative purposes only.
Certain stock imagery © Getty Images.

Editor: Jessica Swift
Cover Art: Katya Buthker

Print information available on the last page.

ISBN: 978-1-9822-4605-1 (sc)
ISBN: 978-1-9822-4606-8 (hc)
ISBN: 978-1-9822-4629-7 (e)

Library of Congress Control Number: 2020906950

Balboa Press rev. date: 10/08/2020

For Maria:

I bring you wherever I go.

CONTENTS

Do *Not* Read This Book

Dear Reader,

When I decided within the first seventy-two hours of caring for Maria that it would be inconceivable for me to be interacting as intimately as I was with her as a *caregiver* and not want to rush home each evening as a *writer* to document every detail to a deliriously meticulous degree, and when, a few months into the job, it became clear that my life purpose at that time was to immortalize Maria and our unlikely relationship in a book, I became a man on two missions. The first mission, as her caregiver, was to keep her alive as long as humanly possible. The second, as a writer, was to do what Hemingway thought writers should do: sit down at a typewriter and bleed.

As I sat there and bled, an action movie began to form. But instead of the plot being driven by exploding cars, it was driven by exploding emotions; instead of being fueled by a flawless hero, it was fueled by an ordinary guy not pretending he cared about anyone but himself. There would be the proverbial ticking clock, but not to count down the amount of time the hero had left to defuse the bomb—it was to indicate the depleting hours until *The Woman in Gold* would be gone forever.

If I fulfilled my mission as a writer, the product of those three years on Danalda Drive would never claim to possess the perfectly polished brushstrokes of a Vermeer painting; instead, it would proudly lay bare the raw and flawed fury of a van Gogh.

So my pledge before I started my work back in 2008 was that whatever blood dripped onto the page I wouldn't judge, I wouldn't clean up, and I wouldn't apologize for. And as a result, you, dear reader, arrived. And because readers like you have become invested in the story over the years, I have just one request before we embark on the continuously colorful unfolding of my life with Maria still in it.

If you have *not* read *The Accidental Caregiver: How I Met, Loved, and Lost Legendary Holocaust Refugee Maria Altmann* (now known as part one), I suggest you set part two aside until you have. Rest assured, this book stands on its own. It is my job as a memoirist to save you a seat in the comfy chair on my shoulder. And while I can reassure you that things will make sense if you don't read part one, so much will be enhanced if you do. I liken parts one and two to a television series—part two is the second season of *The Accidental Caregiver,* and if you ask me, the only true way to get to know Maria is the way I got to know her back in the very first episode: in real time.

Just so we're on the same page, this book is not a new edition of the first book. It's not an addition of any kind. It's not an addendum, an afterword, an appendix, or any other part of the human intestines. It is its own entity—a lot has happened since Maria left.

Okay, dear reader, it's about that time. If you haven't read the original, I will see you back here in good health. Hm. Still here, I see. I like your style. See you in about three seconds.

… two … three … welcome back. Now for some reason Andrea Syrtash, a dating and relationship author and founder of *Pregnantish,* wants to tell you how she spilled a glass of wine on me on a snowy day in 2018.

Then we'll begin.

Foreword

"How I Met Gregor"

On a freezing day in January 2018 at a screening of the movie *Phantom Thread* in Midtown Manhattan, I literally bumped into a man wearing a beautiful white sweater and (unfortunately) sipping a glass of red wine. The wine splattered all over his sweater, and I easily turned the shade of it. He looked me in the eye and said, "Don't worry. I was never into this sweater anyway." I knew I liked this man right then. What I didn't know was how this accident wasn't really an accident. I have no doubt Gregor and I were meant to meet.

Gregor sat down at my table for lunch (because who else would sit with a man at a formal event in a wine-stained sweater?), and we exchanged the usual small talk. He asked me what I did, and I shared that I write books about love. I asked him what he did, and he said, "I wrote a book about love." To be clear, this never happens when I share my job description.

Gregor explained that his book was about the love he had for a ninety-two-year-old Holocaust survivor from Austria. I shared that my father was born in hiding and is a Holocaust survivor from Hungary. As you can imagine, I didn't eat much during this lunch. I wanted to hear more about Gregor's love story.

The title of his book is *The Accidental Caregiver* because when Gregor agreed to be interviewed for the job to care for an elderly woman, he didn't even want the gig. At the time, he was an actor in LA and had no training as a caregiver. He could hardly cook or take care of his own home. But he took the job, and it changed his life. He confided that he had never met, and has still never met, a woman who compares to Maria. He knew from her very first sentence that he loved her.

Knowing that I write and report on love and relationships, Gregor also shared with me that he doesn't understand a lot of women and has a tough time dating because he likes "complicated" women. Some people may have interpreted this to mean that he liked "complicated, demanding divas." (Because, you know, "men love bitches.") But I understood that Gregor meant complicated as in complex—nuanced, interesting, intelligent, and deep. He wanted to find a woman who is paradoxical like Maria was—sexy and strong but also childlike and playful. One who embraced her femininity but who could also hang with the boys. He wanted to find a woman with a sense of humor and a depth of wisdom and kindness, even in her darkest days. This epitomized the love of his life, Maria.

The Daily Mail had captured Gregor's love story in a sensationalistic way (with a click-baity headline like, "Young actor falls for old woman."). But I knew that their love was real. I've always known that true love can transcend time, space, and logic. The very act of trying to define it can diminish it. So trying to explain in words how a young, attractive actor could fall for a robust old lady is tough. Most people won't understand it or believe it.

Gregor and I hugged goodbye. In fact, we were the last to leave the event. I got home and ordered his book and didn't put it down for a week, until I finished it. He brought Maria and their relationship to life so vividly.

I wish I could've met Maria. She and I would have compared notes about Austria and Hungary, about opera and Mozart, and about our love of chestnut puree. We would've swapped jokes and jabs. When I read about Maria through Gregor, she felt like a part of my roots. So much was familiar between our Jewish Austro-Hungarian families (except ours weren't hanging out with Klimt and the Rothschilds). And yet, I'm also aware that that was just Maria. Everyone who met her felt like they knew her.

I'm thrilled that I was a klutz on a snowy January day and that I got to meet Gregor and, through him, Maria. I know you will be as touched by his writing and reflections as I have been. Ultimately, he challenges each of us to consider how many things unfold when we open our hearts to love and possibility—however and wherever they appear. He shows that love and life are not linear or logical, and when you're open to this fact, accidental meetings can change your life.

Andrea Syrtash
January 2020

CHAPTER 1

Dear Reader

Dear reader, I knew I wanted you to get your very own chapter this time around, and I couldn't be more delighted that it's the one that begins our journey.

You should know that not once in the eight years since publishing the first book did I ever have a pining to write a sequel. The three years I spent with Maria Altmann felt like a thousand one-night stands that ended epically at her bedside as she took her final breaths on February 7, 2011. Everything I wanted to say about those thirty-seven months, even everything I could never have imagined I wanted to say, I said in the book. And since I owned the only key ever made, on August 15, 2012, when the book went live on Amazon, I was completely comfortable throwing away the key. It was official: our time together would remain untouched forever.

Then I met the women of WIZO … and everything changed.

In April 2018, a decade after I met Maria, the Women's International Zionist Organization invited me to Australia to embark on a three-week speaking tour—all birthed by a random Facebook message. Suddenly, a sequel was not only about to happen; it was already being written. Because something hit me while hopping around kangaroo-land introducing audiences to (the real) woman in gold: *The Accidental Caregiver* didn't end when Maria died; it only just began.

For years, whenever I reflected on my inscrutable infatuation with Maria, how deep it ran and how insistent it was, I was mostly left befuddled. Why did I love this woman so much? On the surface, everyone who met Maria fell for her. Falling for Maria was like falling for pecan pie—it didn't require any merit. But my love for her felt extraordinary. It went far beneath the surface.

So, dear reader, after ten years of dedicating a large chunk of my life to spreading her joie de vivre around the world, a revelation has dawned ...

My love for Maria never had anything to do with her.

The hundreds of hours I'd spent converting my days as a caregiving neophyte into a Word document that would become a book wasn't so I could prove my love for Maria—it was so I could prove my love to myself. The impassioned depictions I wrote about her in the book weren't to go, "See? I was a caregiver for *the* Maria Altmann." They were actually to go, "See? I can *love*." Though I didn't fully realize it then, my persistent love for Maria was my true nature fighting its way to the surface. At that tender, transitional time in my life as an actor-caregiver, it was simple—if I loved Maria and I fought to show you, dear reader ... then I was living as the real me. If I loved Maria and I kept it to myself, then I wasn't. So part one was quite literally chock-full of the real me.

Sometimes Maria would look at me and say, "I wish I met you seventy years ago." I hated when she said these things because I knew it was genuine, and that hit me like a ton of bricks—because I agreed with her. *I wish I met you too, Maria,* I would bellow to myself but would rarely have the guts to say it aloud. On those one or two times I mustered the courage to say, "I wish I met you too"—requiring a kind of vulnerability that I usually only reserved for acting—it liberated me.

Whether you realize it or not, dear reader, along the journey of the first book, our intimacy was a motivating force for me to keep writing. Now with the second, I want you to know how much I'll rely on you again to be sitting in that comfy chair every step of the way. I realize that at this point you're probably wondering what this journey will entail, and that's okay, because all you really need to know at this moment is that I'll never write *at* you—it will always be *with* you.

Above all I want us both to be inspired to lead with our hearts and pursue what we love in everything we do. I can say that if saying yes to that caregiving job I never wanted in 2008 will cause even one person to say yes to something out of their comfort zone that will end up impacting their life, it was worth it. I've had some illuminating experiences since Maria left, and I'm going to continue to wear my heart on my sleeve as a way to show you my appreciation. We won't agree on everything, and trust me—at times I may not tell you what you want to hear. But I'll always offer a fresh perspective on things.

So welcome to my ten-years-after-I-met-her book and all the accidental offerings that have popped up in my life since Maria packed up and went north—including my chance opportunity to care for her fascinating son in what would turn out to be his last year on Earth, the cross-country journey that guided me to a New York theater to unveil *The Accidental Caregiver* stage play to audiences, my travels to faraway lands like Australia and Mexico to meet Holocaust survivors through my "Love, Maria" events, and virtually every major occurrence in my life in the last eight years. It's not all going to be directly about Maria—sometimes I have to go off alone and feel my way through the darkness—but virtually everything I do seems to lead back to her in some way. Maria's life has somehow become mine.

One more thing, dear reader: scattered throughout this book are select scenes taken from my *Accidental Caregiver* stage play that premiered at the Robert Moss Theater in New York in 2015, as well as imagined conversations with a posthumous Maria. While portions of the exchanges are contrived, they're essentially how we spoke and the things we spoke about, whether sitting in her Cheviot Hills kitchen watching the hummingbirds out her window or shuffling together through her favorite park across the street from the Beverly Hills hotel. Keeping my conversations with Maria going in this sequel has helped me understand myself better, and I hope sharing her playful wit and folksy wisdom can do the same for you.

Speaking of wit and wisdom, let's keep the momentum going with an ode to the Shakespeare in my life.

CHAPTER 2

This Above All

"This above all: To thine own self be true." I was born fated for this line from *Hamlet* to be the soundtrack of my life. But while being true to myself has afforded me respect and helped me better understand my strange and mosaic journey, it has also pushed me down some deeply isolating paths—sometimes inevitable in a world that wants to define you any chance it gets. So before we dive into my undulating days with and without Maria, it feels right that I begin with a quick anecdote that helps us get to know each other more than we already do.

Back in early 2012, during the incipient stages of piecing together part one, I attended a writers' expo at a hotel in Manhattan where authors could pitch their book ideas to literary agents in a speed dating kind of environment. The clock began as you sat down, and you had exactly two minutes to wow them with your million-dollar idea. The day was taxing for me, the buzzing unease of having to prove worthy something I already knew was worthy just by virtue of its existence, and on top of that trying to convince people whose primary job it seemed was to go, "Not for me, thanks," in the most passive-aggressive way possible.

In hindsight, the cards were stacked against me before I even set foot in the hotel. Memoirs are typically the toughest to sell of any genre. It's almost unfair because no one chooses to be a memoirist. It chooses you. And on top of that, it's a nearly impossible way to make a living—it's not as if any aspiring writer, presented with all the ways to make money writing, ever said, "I'll do memoir!"

Fiction writing, on the other hand, is a different animal.

Let me break it down for you in my own terms—to know a memoirist, read his or her book; to know a fiction writer, well, that might take a few in-person get-togethers. While a fiction writer's time is predominantly spent worrying if his or her hard work will bring any lasting success, a memoirist's time is predominantly spent worrying if his or her hard work will bring any lasting peace. Memoirists write for an audience of one (themselves, for their own edification); fiction writers write for an audience of *the more the merrier.* Most memoirists suffer from depression; most fiction writers suffer only from sore fingers. This isn't to imply that memoirists are superior to fiction writers. All (true) writers suffer the same setbacks. But let's just be crystal clear about what memoirists undergo to bring you a product.

Back at the expo, I had a memorable exchange with one agent, we'll call her Debbie. I sat down in her nook, the clock commenced, and I unloaded my fervent description of the book, at that time mostly in outline form and titled *I Just Met a Girl Named Maria.* I was so nervous that my face was sweating, I was short of breath, and I felt myself rambling on and on incoherently.

"So-I-was-this-thirty-two-year-old-actor-who-got-this-job-caring-for-this-ninety-two-year-old-woman-and-it-was-love-at-first-sentence-and-I-quit-everything-I-thought-I-loved-to-be-with-her-and—" I was an oil spill in progress. Eventually, Debbie put a plug in the rig.

"Are there any other narratives?" she asked blithely, as if tired of meeting with authors who had absolutely no idea how to succinctly communicate their thoughts.

"Other narratives?" I was completely shocked by the question. "No. It's just … It's just us having the most entertaining conversations all day long, and we would … I mean, you have to read some of them. It's like a modern-day *Harold and Maude* …"

I was so embarrassed at how unprepared and foolishly emotional

I was getting that I completely shut down and let her close out the session.

"I already love Maria, but no one is going to read a book just about you and this lady," she explained calmly. "It would get claustrophobic. You need more outside narratives to give the reader a breather."

I left Debbie's station with a spinning mind. What she said I couldn't do was exactly what I planned on doing. It was just Maria, me, and whatever the hell came up in conversation. Yes, it was obvious that I needed to work on my elevator pitch, but I kept thinking, *Why am I trying so hard to convince someone of something I already know has value?*

The first takeaway was that you never want to get caught selling anything—exactly what Debbie caught me doing. Bigger than that, though, this wasn't about her being wrong. You could even argue that she was right. But it wasn't her book. Whether readers would resonate with it was actually none of my business. My business was only that I sat down and did it my own way. So I took my outline, turned it into a book, and published it myself.

My point is, success is subjective. It means different things to different people. I've always held steadfast one singular idea of a successful person—someone who follows their passions to become the best at what they care about most. You simply cannot accomplish that living by anyone else's terms.

To thine own self be true.

CHAPTER 3

I Am Not a Caregiver

Before we officially leap off the bow of this ship, let's get one thing straight: I am *not* a caregiver.

I wasn't in 2008 when I cared for Maria, I wasn't in 2013 when I cared for her son Chuck, I wasn't in 2015 when I cared for her cousin Ruth, and I'm not in 2019 as I work on this sequel. Calling myself a caregiver because I cared for Maria would be like calling myself a basketball player because I shot a piece of trash into a trash can. My three years with Maria were a flash in the pan—a pan I never even wanted at first. So it's not: "Oh, he did such an honorable thing caring for that woman." All I did was say yes. Maria took care of the rest.

Most of the time during those three years on Danalda Drive, we weren't so much caregivers as we were hired conversationalists. As a conversationalist, I'd never brought more passion and more work ethic to a "day job" in my entire life. But I cared for Maria knowing that I had the option to pick up and leave—a luxury most career caregivers don't have. The point is, dear reader, if we're meeting for the first time in these first pages, I feel the need to make it clear that I'm not a saint. I don't help most old ladies across the street; I can have a hair-trigger temper; and living in Manhattan now, I want to strangle every slow walker in front of me. I'm not certified, I'm frightened of hospitals, and the only reason I know what a Lorazepam does is because I googled it. (It's a sedative for people having seizures, by the way.)

But I'm not a complete waste of your time, because I do have something deep down in the caves of my soul that I've noticed many career caregivers—and many regular old humans for that matter—don't have. It has nothing to do with certification, training, or a vocation. It's nothing you can touch. So what is it, you ask? A *true* caregiving gene—painted on my bones since birth. Since I can't really define it in one or two sentences, I'm spending the better part of a year writing this book in hopes that by the end you'll know if you have the same gene. If you do, we'll be BFFs.

Now, despite the high degree of respect I have for professional caregivers, there are many I interacted with on Maria's watch who were abrasive, lazy, and cared next to nothing about the person for whom they were "caring." It was appalling but sadly not surprising, considering how little money they make. I don't know what's more revealing about this country: how little caregivers make or how little teachers make. Teachers are molding our youth; caregivers are keeping our elders alive—what could be more worthy of our attention?

In today's world, caregiving as a career is being threatened. Salaries are going up for mostly everyone except members of the care and service industry—how completely insane is that? And with the alarming rate at which technology is consuming our lives, it feels like one day in the near future we won't even bother making eye contact anymore. That means people like Maria will have a harder and harder time finding people like me who are available to keep them young. At least countries like Japan spend billions of dollars a year on technological innovation for the elderly—why many others don't, is a mystery. It reminds me of that quote from Gandhi: "The greatness of a nation and its moral progress can be judged by the way its animals are treated." Swap *elders* for *animals*, and it rings a similar truth.

Look, this isn't a book about how we can get more youth to help our elders, but I'd be remiss not to mention here the only two solutions I see working in a world increasingly ruled by young people: one, get YouTube celebrities to make videos about how important elders are in their lives. If hundreds of millions of youngsters around the world could see their heroes bragging about how totally cool and awesome elders are, how could it not make a dent? The second stems from an article I caught on LinkedIn in the fall of 2019. The headline read something like: "Boy Shields Elder from Rain with Coat." A journalist was actually hired to write an article about a twelve-year-old kid he saw using his coat to keep an elderly lady dry. Can we round up more writers for these? (Call me.)

At any rate, despite having a long way to go before we see elders treated fairly in this country, there is much reason to rejoice. Most people are decent, and life is good, even if the mainstream media makes you think it's all going to hell in a hand basket. So let's enjoy human contact while we still have skin. Let's follow our hearts, let's flee our comfort zones, and let's say *yes*.

In other words, *let's be Maria Victoria Bloch-Bauer Altmann.*

CHAPTER 4

The Glass Wall

At the turn of a gold-speckled door handle, a man in an elegant black dinner suit drifted into an empty white room.

"Here we are, Madame," he said, guiding into the marble-floored quarters a statuesque woman in a violet blouse and white dress pants, a colorful silk scarf daintily draped around her neck.

"Danke, Gustav," said the woman in a fine-drawn Central European accent, seating herself in a chair in the middle of the floor.

"You look particularly snazzy this morning," added Gustav as he went over and fiddled with an electric panel of switches along an otherwise blank wall.

"By the way, Gustav, that movie you showed last week ..."

"*Bride of the Wind?*"

"That was it," the woman said. "I must tell you how very strange it is to see the people you grew up with become a part of history."

A glass panel on the wall suddenly illuminated, showing a giant auditorium with fashionable guests seated around circular tables.

"What are we watching this morning?" the woman asked.

"A gentleman is giving a speech," Gustav answered.

"Which gentleman?" the woman inquired. She studied all the tables facing a stage where a master of ceremonies stood addressing the audience. Her eyes fell on one particular guest. "The man in the blue morning jacket ... at the second table from the left? You see him there?"

"Yes, madame."

"He's rather preoccupied."

"Maybe he's nervous," replied Gustav with a knowing smirk.

"Why would he be nervous?"

"Well, it's not every day one gets to speak to a roomful of people about you." At that, Gustav kissed her right cheek and headed for the door.

"About me?" the woman entreated. "What do you mean *about me?*" She sat there staring through the glass wall at the man in the blue jacket, wondering why she found herself so intrigued by his disinterest.

Suddenly, she gasped. "Gustav!" she shouted with a flourish. "I know who he is! This is who I always tell you about! I haven't seen him in so long! Gustav! Come back here!"

She leapt out of her chair and ran to the glass wall. "My love, can you hear me?" she implored, her nose pressed against the glass like a child watching the early morning snow fall through a bedroom window.

As a lady at the podium finished speaking to boisterous applause, the man in the blue jacket stood up, maneuvered between the tables, and strode confidently onto the stage. He made his way to the microphone, planted his hands heavily on both sides of the podium, and took a deep breath. The room fell silent.

He opened his mouth to speak, but no words came out. His eyes welled up with tears. A collective murmur cascaded through the hall.

"Say something, *Mein Schatz*," appealed the woman behind the glass. "Tell them about the time you came to the house wearing that T-shirt that said Old Navy, and I said, 'But you're too young to be in the Old Navy.' You remember that, darling?! Can you hear me?! Or that time when that big, ugly jalopy cut us off on Pico Boulevard, and I flipped her the bird, and I looked over at you, pointed to my raised middle finger, and said: '*This* is a wonderful thing.' She giggled. "You loved that. We had fun together."

As if hearing her voice, the man at the podium laughed through his tears and managed to gaze down at the expectant faces for the first time.

"Now if you had pulled me aside in January of 2008," he began, "and you said, 'Okay, Gregor, in two weeks, three things are going to happen to you: You're gonna become a caregiver for a ninety-two-year-old woman, you're gonna fall in love with her, and it will significantly alter the course of your life, I would have been nuts not to think you weren't nuts ...'"

As the man at the podium continued with this speech, the woman, her eyes never leaving him, slowly backed away from the glass wall and returned to her seat. A box of tissues appeared before her. "Thank you," she said as she pulled one out to dab her eyes.

"You're welcome," replied a red-faced Gustav, who had been standing there the whole time.

Gustav and the statuesque woman watched as the man behind the glass paused and then looked straight up at them.

He blew a kiss.

She blew one back.

CHAPTER 5

Maria the Magnificent

On an unseasonably balmy fall afternoon in Melbourne at a brunch in a brimming banquet hall, 250 sets of eyes sat laser-focused on the speaker behind the podium.

All was quiet.

It was so quiet you could hear a yarmulke drop.

There was just one tiny problem: the speaker couldn't speak.

Of all the things that could have gone wrong in Oz, dear reader, losing my ability to speak was not one the Women's International Zionist Organization or I ever considered. I had spent the last few weeks dry running my PowerPoint presentation in my Hell's Kitchen apartment preparing to be keynote speaker—the first time in my life being given that honor—at a lavish brunch at the famed Crown Melbourne. I practiced in front of everyone from my warmest friends to my most impartial acquaintances, the latter of which included a curmudgeon named Stewart I'd met at a screening of the movie *Florence Foster Jenkins* who seemed to have an issue with everything. He sat there scowling on my black leather couch the whole time and then miraculously came up with positive things to say. It was officially bulletproof.

And it's not like I was kicking it off with something heavy. I had planned on announcing to my new Aussie friends that I, just the previous day on a trip to Phillip Island, had officially checked "take selfie with kangaroo" off my bucket list. It was meant to be less a knee-slapper than a sufficient icebreaker, and it was, frankly, a bit of a gamble considering kangaroos to Aussies are like squirrels to

Americans—more pests than pets. At that point, however, in the throes of my unruly stutterings, I was more worried about being escorted off stage than bombing my tepid kangaroo quip. So I continued my fight to get to that damn quip. But the harder I fought, the further away I got from being able to speak. And I'm pretty sure *able to speak* was a deciding factor in my being hired for the *speaking* tour.

But it turns out that I had a ticket out of this predicament: *The Woman in Gold.* I knew she was up there peering through that glass wall, giving me the go-ahead to face that flood like a man—a man who suddenly didn't care he'd left his umbrella back in New York. Here I was in congenial-land, 10,000 miles away, for damn good reason. So I sprinted into that storm to find Maria smiling as wide as the 405 Freeway, standing there in her cashmere sweater and silk scarf ready to set me free. If I was going to cry my eyes out, I was going to do it across the universe in front of 250 folks I had never met. So I cried one of those primordial cries with a passion for Maria so unexplainable that the words I couldn't find could never have done it justice anyway.

But seriously, dear reader—what the heck was I thinking, crying in front of all those impeccably dressed strangers? Didn't I owe them better? There was absolutely no indication I would be bawling my eyes out up there. In my hotel a couple hours earlier, I spoke jubilantly with Maria as I stood in front of the mirror in my gray dress pants and blue sport jacket.

"What do you think?" I asked her as if she were there watching me get ready.

"Absolutely fabulous," she replied with that oft-blazing fire in her eyes and that thing she'd love to do to show her approval—connecting her thumb to her forefinger to make the okay gesture. Then she secretly looked me up and down, but c'mon, Maria made her affection for me as plain as day. Somehow she never had any clue how obvious it always came across.

"You'll have all the ladies swooning with that morning jacket," Maria asserted with faux civility. *Morning jacket,* by the way, was an old European term for a sport jacket. Her father used to use it. The term—and how adorably surprised she would get when I would tell her people stopped saying it after 1940—would have me giggling like a schoolboy, which inevitably had her giggling like a schoolgirl. We went back and forth like this in the hotel room mirror until I was certain that the sport coat I had bought at the H&M Store on Forty-Eighth and Fifth in New York was the greatest morning jacket ever made. Then I said to her: "So does this mean I'm not allowed to wear it at *night?*" That was my go-to joke, which always set her over the edge.

After I explained to the audience that the only reason I took the caregiving job was because Maria opened up her mouth, that formidable flood started chasing me again as I thought of that moment when I heard her tender, lilting accent for the first time—an impossibly enchanting cross between Maria from *The Sound of Music* and legendary chef Julia Child. It's a moment I describe in the first book as "love at first sentence."

But the best cries are the cries you never see coming. And once I allowed myself to let it go a second time, I felt, at least in those moments when the audience was on the edge of their seats feeling everything I was feeling, that I was fully living my purpose; I was right where I was supposed to be. Why I was doing it was a mystery. But the architect Frank Gehry said that "if you know what you're going to do in advance, you won't do it." And that was the lesson in Melbourne, maybe even of this entire book: the thing about following a heart is that you don't need to know why ... you just need to do it.

The warm audience wasn't just dumb luck. This had nothing to do with the gregariousness of the Australian people. This was the penetrating spirit of Maria Victoria Bloch-Bauer Altmann making sure that wherever I went on her behalf was exactly where I was supposed to be and with whom I was supposed to be with.

CHAPTER 6

The Ice Cream Parlor

In addition to the stage play that premiered in New York in 2015—a theater adventure I'll relive with you later in the book—I adapted *The Accidental Caregiver* into a feature film script, a film I intend to make one day as a kind of modern-day *Harold and Maude*. This chapter holds an excerpt from that film script. When I first got the job with Maria, I struggled with the fact that I came to Hollywood to be an actor, not a caregiver. In my mind, there was no way I could be taken seriously by anyone of influence in the entertainment industry by essentially admitting that I was a male nurse.

Grant is me, by the way. All other names are real. I'm often asked why I didn't name him Gregor—or play him, for that matter. I think it was because, first of all, living it in real life was enough, and second of all, I wanted to see if new insights could unfold with a different name and a different person. That, and by the time we put up the play, I was ... too old to play myself!

Interior. Ice Cream Parlor—Afternoon

Maria and Grant lean over the counter, ogling at all the decadent flavors.

GRANT, *to Maria.* I wonder if Chanel makes a flavor.
MARIA. How did you know I like Chanel?

GRANT. Lily told me.

MARIA, *suddenly jealous.* When did you speak to Lily?

A teenage employee sidles up.

MARIA. Lily is very boring, darling. You don't want anything to do with her. And did you know she'll be 98 in October? Not such a spring chicken anymore.

GRANT. Well you're ninety—

MARIA, *intentionally cutting him off.* Mein schatz, this lovely young man wants to take our order. (*Now speaking to the employee.*) Do you have Chanel?

EMPLOYEE. Let me go check with my boss.

GRANT. She's joking, man. Two Oreo cookie cups and two waters.

MARIA. Oh, I don't drink water, darling. Fish fuck in it.

GRANT. Great. I'm never drinking water again. And neither is he.

Employee gets the ice cream. Grant takes Maria's arm and leads her to a table.

MARIA. Look how elegant you are.

GRANT. Stop saying that. I know, I know, it's the "real me." Mr. Elegant. Whatever.

Employee brings them their ice cream.

MARIA, *to employee.* Thank you, sweetheart. (*To Grant.*) What's wrong? You seem a little ornery today.

GRANT. Ornery? I'm fine.

MARIA. I haven't seen this side of you yet. It's sort of titillating. (*Scoops her ice cream.*) This is delicious. You need to try it.

GRANT. I guess I'm a little frustrated I haven't heard from my agent. I feel unproductive.

MARIA. What is it that you like about acting?

GRANT. I don't know. Being in the moment with someone. Being fearless. Being exposed.

MARIA. Like we always are.

She clasps his hand.

MARIA. My husband wanted so much to be an opera singer. He had a beautiful voice, but in those days, there weren't nearly as many opportunities as there are today. I tried to use our family connections to help him. I even arranged a meeting with Arturo Toscanini, the biggest conductor of the time. But sadly, nothing led anywhere. It crushed him that he never fully realized his dreams. He always felt like an outsider who couldn't quite get on the inside. It's a tough business. It's all who you know—it's never changed. I feel for you, I really do.

Grant quickly yanks his hand away.

GRANT. What's that supposed to mean?

MARIA. What did I say?

GRANT. "I feel for you." I don't need your pity, Maria. I know this business is tough. You always go out of your way to make sure I know that.

MARIA. I wasn't pitying you, darling. I was offering—

GRANT. And, I mean, why do you feel for me? I can take care of myself.

Maria is completely stunned at Grant's outburst.

MARIA. I want the best for you. I love you.

GRANT. You don't love me! And stop implying I'm not good enough to make it. That whole Fritz analogy. I'm not your husband, okay? I'm an outsider who *will* make it on the inside.

A silent moment.

MARIA. Why are you so reluctant to accept good in your life?

GRANT. I had plenty of good in my life before I took this job. I should never have … The point is, I'm good enough. My acting is respected and admired, and I'm not like everybody else. All the people who told me no, who ignored me, who doubted me will be sorry, including you. I don't need this stupid job anyway!

He stands and announces to the patrons.

GRANT. I'm not a caregiver, okay?!

He throws the keys on the table.

GRANT, *to Maria.* Find a new Morgan Freeman.

Grant storms out of the parlor.
Smash cut to:

Vienna, 1938—Dachau Concentration Camp. Night.

Maria's husband, Fritz, walks down a dirt road littered with prisoner tents.
Smash cut back to:

Present Time

Grant walks briskly down the sidewalk.
Back to:

Dachau—Continuous

Fritz starts to run down the dirt road ...
Smash cut to:

Present Time

Grant starts to run into the street.
Back to:

Dachau

Fritz full on sprints. He's being chased by two SS officers waving sticks.

SS Officer. Prisoner escape! Prisoner escape! Prisoner C-33 has escaped!

Fritz is jumped from behind by the SS men. They start beating him.

Present Time

Cars honk and screech to avoid Grant. He emits a primordial scream.

Grant. Ahhhhhhhhhhhhhhhhhhhhhh!

Back to:

Dachau

The SS men have left Fritz writhing in agony on the ground.

Present Time

Grant, dripping in sweat, catches his breath and walks back to the ice cream parlor. Cut to:

Outside Ice Cream Parlor

Grant watches Maria through the window still seated quietly in the same spot. He walks into the parlor. She looks up at him.

MARIA. You're all wet.

She takes a napkin from the table and wipes his forehead. She hands him the keys. He helps her out of the chair, and they exit in silence.

CHAPTER 7

Kathryn the Great

One of the blessings of my relationship with Maria was that it was so perfectly uncomplicated. My troubles seemed to magically vanish when I stepped out of my Toyota Scion and into her house each morning. Just simply sitting with each other at the table at breakfast watching the hummingbirds drink from the feeder was all we needed to feel that life made perfect sense.

Conversely, my relationship with my mother, Kathryn, has been complicated my entire life. We made significant strides in 2019—a long time coming. I'd like to introduce you to her in this chapter, and ensuing chapters. First, it's interesting to note that back in 2007, about a year before I met Maria (I was about thirty-two), my mom, an art history major from Vassar College, showed me a book containing paintings by an artist named Gustav Klimt. I had never heard of him before and became enthralled with the dazzling *Gold Portrait*. Little did I know that twelve months later I'd be meeting the woman (Maria) whose uncle commissioned Klimt to paint many of the pictures in that very book. Talk about foreshadowing.

Here's what I know about my mother's childhood from the few times she's been in the headspace to "go there" with me: She grew up on the South Side of Chicago in the 1950s—at that time one of the most dangerous neighborhoods in America. Her Czech father was an alcoholic, her Sicilian mother had a sixth-grade education, and her brothers never even graduated from high school and were in and out of jail most of their lives. With no role models and a pittance allowance, Kathryn looked forward to two things as a youth: scrounging up enough pocket change to buy penny candy at the corner bodega, and occasionally getting to go to a White Sox game at Comiskey Park. There she would enjoy a Chicago dog: a hot dog with American mustard, diced onions, and, her favorite ingredient: fresh tomatoes.

In early 2019, on a visit to her condo in Reston, Virginia, we were at a grocery store and she threw a package of hot dogs into the cart—I had never seen her do that. Turns out she had a craving for a classic Chicago dog. Of course, she had to buy the tomatoes to make it truly authentic.

"Tomatoes on a hot dog?" I asked skeptically.

She insisted I try. Look, all a hotdog needs is mustard for me to devour it.

About her dad, she told me one story.

"My dad always brought home fresh whitefish from the deli down the street." To this day, thinking about whitefish chokes her up. It was touching to see that despite what surely must have been a tumultuous relationship with a man struggling with alcoholism, my mother chose this memory to relive. She can rarely go into a supermarket without bringing whitefish home.

Of her mother, she had three things. The first: "My mother would chase me around the house and threaten to kill me."

The second was a story about a trip to a clothing store. When my mom was around five, her mom was pushing her around a clothing store in a stroller. At one point, she noticed her mom take an item of clothing off the racks and sneak it into the stroller, covering it up with a blanket. They rolled out without paying for it.

The third was her only positive memory of her mother: "She used to make this fresh marinara sauce we would put over pasta. It was the best I ever tasted." Penny candy, Chicago dogs, whitefish, and marinara sauce—I didn't realize it before writing them all down together that every one of her brightest memories as a kid is related to food. Well, except this last one.

Mom wasn't particularly close to her brothers, but she has a story about one, John, on a day he showed up at the house with a brand-new Cadillac. She had just gotten her driver's license, and John let her drive his new baby down the street. Halfway around the block she lost control and banged it into a tree. She was unhurt, but the Cadillac's front end wasn't. She left the car and walked home, prepared for a tongue-lashing.

"John never got upset," she said to me, her eyes welling up. "He was like: 'It's just a car.'"

She downplays her childhood a lot, but I know it's because the painful memories are too much to bear. And being a positive, God-fearing woman, her natural instinct is to open, not close, a window. But it must have been absolute hell for her to cause her to run away from home so young.

She ran away when she was sixteen, and never returned and never spoke to anyone in her family again. At eighteen she got a job at the *Wall Street Journal* in New York City while living on Christopher Street in the West Village. During the summers, she waitressed at the now defunct Lobster Inn in Southampton, and with the money she saved, she put herself through Vassar College, graduating cum laude one class ahead of actor Meryl Streep. At age twenty-five, she met my dad, Keith, and for the ensuing three decades worked in education, managing college prep centers in the Washington, DC, area. My parents divorced when I was twenty-one.

A decade ago, at age sixty-two, she started her own financial planning business focusing on retirement plan insurance. She gives seminars at restaurants around Northern Virginia. Today, she works with the #1 FMO (Field Marketing Organization) in the entire country, thereby making her one of the top 50 Fixed Index Annuity producers in America. There is no rational reason my mother should have had made it out of her formative years alive. She is a self-made woman in every way.

"No one ever gave me anything growing up," my mom told my brother Christian and me once. "So I am on this Earth to give you guys everything."

Over the years, we've tumbled down the deepest wells and climbed up the highest mountains. We've been best friends, and we've been worst enemies, out of the woods one moment, and a few moments later back in the forest completely lost.

I look at her now, and I'm in awe of what she's accomplished in life. I brag to my friends about her all the time. Yet none of the things I've always held in reverence of her ever brought any lasting peace to our relationship. For my entire life, it was a mystery. If I'm being honest, it still is.

But in 2019 something happened that set our relationship on a new path.

CHAPTER 8

Woman in Gold

During brunch at the Crown, I shared a joke with the audience Maria told me once that I never put in the first book. In retrospect, if I had just sat her down one day and insisted she tell me every joke she'd ever heard, I would have had a third book in the series: *Jokes I've Heard*, by Maria Altmann.

So there's this guy in a mad rush driving through a parking garage searching for a spot. Every spot is full. Row after row. I mean, he's gotta be somewhere now. *He gets so desperate that he throws his car in park and says: Look, Lord, I know I haven't been your most faithful servant over the years, but I need a parking spot right now, and if you open one up for me, I promise I'll love you and honor you for the rest of my life. Suddenly, a spot opens. Right in front of him! He's beside himself. He looks up and says: Forget it. I found one!*

Not bad, eh? The audience certainly thought so. I explained that the day I met Maria in 2008—at least when I reflected on what that day meant as I was piecing together my presentation—felt like a parking spot opening up for me.

With a PowerPoint showing never-before-seen pictures of Maria from her childhood in Austria to her adulthood in California, the audience witnessed Vienna's heyday through Maria's eyes, when it was the artistic and cultural center of the world, as well as got a play-by-play of her escape from Austria with her husband, Fritz. But at the heart of the talk were the personal anecdotes about our playful rapport and her trademark puckish wit.

I told them that when I first started working for Maria I invited her to the premiere of a film I starred in called *Night Before the Wedding,* which had a lot of swear words. I went up to her afterward in the dark theater and asked, "Could you hear it okay?"

She replied without hesitation, "I heard every *fucking* word."

I had to pause a good ten seconds so the laughter in the banquet hall could die down.

Another story I told was about a time when Maria and I were at the Beverly Hills hotel to have lunch with Stephen Lash, the chairman of Christie's—the auction house that in 2006 sold four of the Klimts owned by Maria's Uncle Ferdinand Bloch-Bauer. (The fifth painting, the *Gold Portrait*, was sold in a private sale to Billionaire Philanthropist Ronald Lauder for $135 million, at that time the highest price ever paid for a work of art).

Anyway, while we were waiting for Stephen in the lobby, Actor Michael Douglas walked by and stopped at the front desk. Maria recognized him right away and couldn't stop gushing about him. I convinced her to let me introduce her. Under immense protest (as if she were meeting the star quarterback in high school), I led her to him as he was leaving the front desk for the elevators. He stopped, I said I had a friend who wanted to meet him, and in no time Michael Douglas and Maria Altmann were talking about Austria and art. She couldn't resist calling him and his father "fabulous" every three seconds. When the pleasant exchange ended, Michael said goodbye and went to push the elevator button. That's when Maria leaned into my ear and yelled (thinking she had whispered): "*He's so short!*" This would have been completely okay … if he hadn't heard it.

I'm not kidding when I tell you that the legendary Michael Douglas stopped dead in his tracks, and like a scene right out of *Romancing the Stone*, he cocked his head slightly to the side to display that famous jawline. Then, for me at least, time screeched to a halt. I stood there completely frozen, my mouth probably wide open.

Please don't turn around, Michael, I silently begged to myself. *I didn't tell her to say that.* Thankfully, he never turned around. The elevator doors opened, and he disappeared. *Exhale.* I was still so embarrassed that he heard her, but at least we didn't have to endure the agonizing awkwardness of a confrontation. Stephen got a royal kick out of it when we sat down to lunch. The audience rumbled with laughter throughout this entire telling. The biggest laughs of the afternoon. (Funnily enough, at a subsequent event in Mexico, a guy came up to me afterward and told me his wife met Michael Douglas in Russia, and the first thing she said after he walked away was, "He's so short!" No doubt she whispered it like a normal person.)

I showed the audience visuals from my days producing reality television and working as an actor before I met Maria. I told them how I'd driven out to Hollywood not knowing a single soul other than this one dude—Greg Normart, who's a good friend now—I was interviewing with for a television show called *Blind Date*. And then how when I first became an actor I landed a job as a caterer at the Music Center in Los Angeles. I said to the audience, "I don't know if any of you know this, but when you become an actor, you get a job in the food industry." It was intended to be a truth, but they decided it was a joke. It was definitely both.

Maria's escape from Austria inspired many of the guests to share with me their own escapes stories. How could it be, I wondered, that a self-absorbed actor who had taken a caregiving job he never even wanted, who was about as Jewish as Mike Pence, was the *keynote speaker* at a function in a country that, outside of Israel, is said to have the largest Holocaust community in the world? As nonsensical as it sounded, there I was, sitting at the foot of a long, looping queue of survivors and children of survivors who couldn't wait to speak to me.

I had many memorable exchanges at my signing table. During one, a woman named Rita told me that she was a prisoner at Treblinka Extermination Camp as a little girl. One morning she was sent with a group to be gassed. As they huddled in the showers, the gas ducts malfunctioned, and they were forced to wait there until they were fixed.

The ducts never got fixed properly, and the only way I was sure of that was because all four feet, two inches of resolute Rita was standing with the most dignified erectness telling me about it!

On another encounter, after I signed a book for a man named David, he pulled out of his pocket a black opal ring, handed it to me, and said simply, "Thank you." He bowed and walked away with his book, saying nothing else. I wear it every day with pride.

Many guests who had entered the brunch having seen *Woman in Gold*—the movie where Helen Mirren portrays Maria in her fight to get the Klimt paintings back from Austria—expressed to me that while they enjoyed the film, they never felt like they got to know who Maria really was—my appearance that afternoon in Melbourne filled that void. There were a handful of historical and anecdotal inaccuracies in the film, and I could have spent time pointing them out, but it was much more interesting to talk about who Maria was *outside* of her depiction in the film.

While Helen Mirren's "steely" Maria worked sufficiently on screen for a wide audience who never met her, do you know what worked better for me personally, dear reader? Maria *Altmann's* "tender" Maria—the *real* Maria I hugged and kissed every morning for three years. In real life, Maria was a basket of Golden Retriever puppies left out on a sunny country porch. You'd never experience the full extent of this while watching Mirren's portrayal. Maria had that Mirren steely side, but it was taking a power nap until she absolutely had to use it for things like dealing with the *still* anti-Semitic Austrian government. Even at Maria's steeliest, though, that basket of puppies was always resting on the porch ready to shower you with wet licks.

Mirren's innate austere British-ness still gave us certain attributes of the real Maria: her fortitude, her gentility, and in some scenes a taste of her Churchill-esque wit. But the Maria I knew smiled giddily from ear to ear the moment she opened her eyes in the morning. She thanked restaurant valets multiple times just for handing her keys back. She spoke to her Mexican housemaid like she would speak to her own daughter. And she would sit across from me at breakfast Monday mornings wearing her lime-green bathrobe and her impish grin, wondering if I had been naughty over the weekend. (Odds were that I had, which delighted her even more.)

Maria's boundlessly affectionate side largely missing from the movie was essentially by design—for example, the screenwriter conveniently left out the fact that Maria had four loving children. It makes Hollywood sense, at least. *The strong-willed widow* sounds much more compelling and dramatic than *the loving mother of four children.* But what people don't get from the movie is that Maria's uncompromising joie de vivre, not her heroic journey to recover the Klimt paintings, is her true legacy. This fact will not be overlooked in *The Accidental Caregiver* feature film. But I want to make clear that the fact that the movie was made in the first place was a blessing for everyone. It's too bad Maria wasn't around to see it, even though she always had a hard time believing she was worthy of any accolades.

Because the movie chronicles Maria's fight to recover the Klimt paintings, I'm in the unique position to tell people about many other fascinating aspects you could never find in movies or history books— like the major hand she played in introducing cashmere and argyle to America in 1947. The cashmere sweater folded in your closet right now exists in part because of Bernhard and Maria's work in California after the war.

As you may recall from the first book, before Hitler's annexation of Austria in 1938, Maria's brother-in-law Bernhard Altmann owned successful wool factories in Vienna that manufactured cashmere and argyle. These were two fabrics that America had barely heard of before 1947. Three days after Hitler first rode in his topless jeep through the streets of Vienna, on March 11, 1938, Bernhard's brother Fritz— Maria's husband—was arrested and thrown on the first bus to Dachau Concentration Camp. While Fritz remained in the camp, Maria was at home working out a deal with the Nazis that would force Bernhard to sign his cashmere business over to the National Socialists in exchange for his younger brother's release. Six weeks into Fritz's imprisonment at Dachau, the deal was solidified and Fritz was freed. In surrendering his textile business, Bernhard lost everything he had ever worked for in life.

Over the next decade, Bernhard fled the Nazis and opened up factories in Liverpool and Fall River, Massachusetts, but neither mill had any lasting success. It looked unlikely Bernhard would ever achieve the same heights he had before the Anschluss. In 1947, both branches permanently shut their doors. With nothing really left to lose, Bernhard mailed Maria a package in California containing a cashmere sweater and a pair of argyle socks with the note: "See what you can do with these in California." Maria took the package to Kerr's Department store in Beverly Hills (no longer there), asked for the buyer, and showed him the two textiles. As Maria explained to me, "He said five words to me that any salesman would dream of hearing—'How. Many. May. We. Buy?'" Those five words set their lives in a new direction.

Bernhard eventually became Bernhard Altmann Cashmere, opening up a factory in Texas that would become a multimillion-dollar empire. Eventually, one in every three cashmere sweaters sold in America came from his Texas mill. Only once in the thirty-seven months I knew Maria did she call anyone a genius. That was reserved for Bernhard. (I have since written up Bernhard's Wikipedia entry—read more about his fascinating life as new contributors fill in more and more interesting details.)

To me, Maria is a genius. She grew up in excessive opulence yet spent a lifetime appreciating the value of a dollar. She was instrumental in gaining the Gestapo's trust so that she and her husband, Fritz, could escape. She battled an entire nation, along with her lawyer Randy Schoenberg, and won, paving the way for other families to sue governments for looted belongings. And she did it all with a breezy elegance and charm. This was no ordinary 92-year-old woman. I still hear her explosive guffaws and her lilting voice often, her *my love*s and her *my darling*s dancing in my head like vocal sugarplums.

CHAPTER 9

Come Spring

I was instructed that on April 26, 2018, when my Qantas flight touched down in Melbourne for the launch of the speaking tour, a short-statured woman holding a sign with my name on it would be waiting for me at the baggage claim. As I stepped into the baggage claim imagining lifting up my dead eyes to meet the gaze of a lustrous woman donning a majestic sign ready to whisk me off in my stretch limo, there was no woman in sight. My flight was on time. Something wasn't right.

I made my way down the line of lookers reuniting with their loved ones, and I, with no one claiming me as a loved one, suddenly felt as if I owed them all an explanation. *I'm a very important person, you see, and there was supposed to be a …* I mused in my head as I anxiously pulled out my phone, circling around trying to connect to the free airport Wi-Fi I had been enjoying just minutes ago. It wasn't finding it anymore. I couldn't send or receive any messages to Dione, the executive director at the WIZO office. I needed to be at the office ASAP to help work out the PowerPoint kinks before Sunday's brunch. *Crikey!*

I ambled off to the other end of the concourse to find a seat and figure out what to do next. En route, I passed a woman in a business suit leaning against the wall staring ahead indifferently. Propped up on the wall next to her was a large piece of white cardboard with a name written in black magic marker: Gregor Collins. The name sounded vaguely familiar. We both exploded with laughter about how my sign holder, whose one job it was to stand there and hold up a sign for me, decided to walk off and forget about me! Turned out, this "lowly" sign holder was the president of WIZO Melbourne, Helen Granek. The president personally picking me up at the airport—and clearly having a sense of humor—was the first sign of blessings to come.

When we arrived at the pickup area, I met Kiwi Carol—my admittedly lame nickname for her after learning she is from New Zealand—behind the wheel of a whirring Toyota (not quite a limo), and after I shared stories about my intractable sweet tooth, they swung by a coffee shop serving delectable pastries. They made certain I knew Melbourne had the best coffee in the world. "The best coffee in New York is from Aussie-run coffeehouses," Carol informed me, a tip I couldn't wait to try upon my return to the Big Apple. We didn't have much time to dillydally. I had to dump my bag off at my hotel and head to the office.

When I set foot in the office, it felt even more like home than my own apartment in New York. Every person I met felt like a friend. Maria was continuing to bless me with something I've searched for my entire life: family I could touch. Because I had Skyped mostly with Dione—working together for months ironing out the details of the brunch event—meeting her in person for the first time felt like catching up with a BFF. WIZO Employees started coming out of the woodwork: Ruth, Shelley, Chavivah—like Maria, they were all lights turned to the brightest setting. And they loved Maria just like I loved her! I was being handed computer printouts, almond pastries (how did they know), and taking selfies with the office staff—getting down to business never felt so right. And to think two hours prior I was on a flight I thought would last until I died either of natural causes or from watching too many Ed Helms movies.

The next day, April 27—the day before the big "Love, Maria" brunch at the Crown—Dione took me to Phillip Island to help me check "take selfie with kangaroo" off my Oz list. When we entered the farm carrying our little paper bags of goodies to feed to the 'roos, happy, hopping, hungry ones circled us almost immediately. There were small ones, which were wallabies, and large ones, which were scary—I'm six foot two, and I swear a couple of them towered over me on their hind legs.

The most unnerving part was when they propped up on their sledgehammer feet to eat snacks out of our palms. Unbeknownst to them, their razor-sharp claws would dig into our skin while they got to their surprisingly gentle nibbling. At one point, Dione snapped a picture of me hand-feeding an emu while a kangaroo with a joey in its pouch waited patiently in line. Before my trip, someone had told me that Tasmanian devils were fictional. According to them, they only existed in Bugs Bunny cartoons. I believed him until I saw one taking a nap on its belly.

Dione's Mum Mira took me to the beautiful Melbourne Botanical Gardens where wild kookaburras and cockatoos flitted about. By the end of the day, I was calling her my Australian mother. Kiwi Carol played tour guide for me, a fitting task for someone who was also a part-time Uber driver. She was my right-hand donut lover and took me to all the best donut shops, including the Bistro Morgan, run by a seventeen-year-old kid named Morgan Hipworth, who, as the story goes, rises every morning at dawn to fry five hundred doughnuts before school.

The day after the brunch I was invited to the Melbourne Jewish Centre, a museum founded by Holocaust survivors in the 1950s. In lieu of possessing anything resembling justifiable credentials for being labeled a special guest at a Holocaust museum, all I could do was represent Maria not as Maria the Holocaust survivor, not as Maria the Klimt painting owner, but as Maria the character out of a great novel. What made this museum so special was that survivors—the founders—roamed the hallways on any given day. Anna, the gracious museum curator who took me around to all the sections, said things like, "You see that man standing over there by the front desk?" Then she'd point to a picture on the wall. "This is his brother." It made the afternoon deeply personal.

Before I continued to new adventures, I was introduced to a Polish survivor of the Warsaw Ghetto named, coincidentally, Maria, who had written a book called *Come Spring*. The way she signed it for me reminded me of *my Maria*, her soft, bony fingers wavering with each pen stroke. The entire time Melbourne Maria and I spoke she had the biggest smile plastered on her face, and whenever someone new would walk by—whether a member of the staff or a patron off the street—she would turn to them unsolicited, exclaiming, "Everyone is so good to me! I can't believe it! I'm so lucky!"

Melbourne Maria, at ninety-five years young, was having the time of her life.

CHAPTER 10

Girl in the Sundress

As I stood at the podium, I just couldn't quite believe she was actually sitting in the audience. I didn't know exactly where, but I knew she was out there somewhere, because we'd been texting the last few weeks about her attending. Before those texts, though, we had lost touch for seven years. You know this girl from the first book. I referred to her in its epilogue—where I chronicled my trip to Austria after Maria died in 2011—as "Girl in the Sundress." Our chance encounter in 2011 in Budapest was like something right out of the movie *Before Sunrise*. We met randomly on a crowded train, exchanged numbers, parted ways, met up later, danced the night away, and ended up lip-locked on an abandoned roof in Pest. Needless to say we didn't get much sleep that night.

Fast forward to early 2018—a few weeks before my tour Down Under—and we hadn't spoken since that fateful day in Budapest seven years earlier. I sent her a random text to say hello and to tell her I had written a book and included a section about meeting her on my post-Maria trip to Europe. *Was it even a working number?* She texted me back, as happy to hear from me as I was from her. And she knew all about the book—we'd been connected on Facebook over the years without either of us realizing it. I mentioned I was going to Australia on a speaking tour in April and jokingly suggested that she fly in from Budapest to attend.

Her reply, dear reader? "I live in Melbourne." When those words lit up on my phone, I could have sworn she was playing around—she definitely wasn't. Wow. Of all the places in the world she could have ended up, she ended up in *Melbourne?* From *Budapest?* Since the tickets to my talk were $150, I felt uncomfortable asking her to buy one, so I insisted we have a coffee when I was in town. She demanded she attend the brunch. One hundred and fifty dollars to hear me speak sounded to her like a deal. Then she immediately bought another ticket for a friend before even finding out if she was available.

After every single book sold out at the brunch (and more needed to be ordered), all that remained was the red-faced Girl in the Sundress, who I hadn't even spoken to in person yet, standing demurely across the room watching me sign books and shake hands with sparkly-eyed strangers. I kept looking over at her and seeing her giggle. I couldn't wait to walk over.

When I finished signing the books, we met halfway and embraced. Neither of us could find any real words. Everything had already been said seven years ago. We walked hand in hand out of the Crown, on some kind of magical cloud. We traded side-eyes, headshakes and exhales, wistfully wondering what our lives could have been had I decided not to get on that bus from Vienna bound for Prague in 2011. What if I had stayed behind with her? What if she had come with me back to LA? So many fantastical scenarios to consider, but in our minds there was only one worth clinging onto: if my noncommittal American ass had stayed, we would have ended up together. She had married a traditional Hungarian man, as I always imagined she deserved.

Our hands stayed clasped as we walked in step along the Yarra River—seven years earlier we had done the same thing along the Danube. And just as our time together had been limited when we first met, history was repeating itself in Melbourne, but the moments brought nary an urgency, only a sense that the *now* we found ourselves in would last as long as our hearts wanted it to. Girl in the Sundress and I weren't living our lives on a straight line, we were along Nietzsche's flat circle, going around and around again and again, the journey of two forces, two tails of energy undulating next to each other. We were meant to meet in Budapest, meant to meet again here in Oz seven years later, and we were meant to meet in … well, where *would* we meet next on the circle of life?

"What now?" she asked after we'd been strolling aimlessly for a while.

I suggested we trek to my hotel at St. Kilda Beach.

Before she could respond, I fervidly told her about the fairy penguins that apparently congregated on the rocks by the beach right outside my hotel every sundown—you know, just in case I had to give her an incentive to come with me. She found this amusing. *No sale needed, Gregor.* We rode the bus mostly in comfortable silence.

When we arrived at St. Kilda, we walked down the pier out to the edge where the penguins shivered between the rocks after a full day of fishing on the high seas. We honored the signs telling us not to use the flash on our cameras. Apparently it hurt their precious little eyes.

At sundown, we walked to my hotel room. We both sat down on the bed, clasped our hands, and then in unison fell on our backs as if on a blanket in an open field gazing up at the stars. I felt Hurricane Katrina coming with a force like it had at the Crown earlier, but I had no fight left and allowed my tears to flow.

"It's been an emotional day for you with Maria and all," she offered, taking my sleeve and helping me wipe my tears with it. It wasn't only Maria who was making me emotional; it was GITSD—my inability to commit to her all those years ago, and my inability to commit to anyone in a long time.

When I had been faced with the prospect of committing to Maria, I said yes unequivocally. When faced with the prospect of committing to the Girl in the Sundress, why couldn't I say yes?

See you in another seven years, Adrienne.

CHAPTER 11

The Darkness

It's a big mystery why darkness persists for me, sometimes in flashes, sometimes over the course of an entire day. I have a good life, I have people who love me, and I'm learning more and more to accept myself. In this chapter I'm impelled to experiment with how Maria might help me through some of these ephemeral dark stretches. She was an expert at turning a somber subject into a fun one instantaneously—with me, it's often the other way around.

———◆◆———

MARIA. What's wrong, darling?

GREGOR. I was just thinking. You never got to see some things about me. Sides you probably wouldn't like.

MARIA. Well, I did see your profile. I miss looking at your face.

GREGOR. Not that kind of side.

MARIA. Like what, my love?

GREGOR. I don't know. Darknesses. But it didn't matter, I guess.

MARIA. Everybody has darknesses, my love.

GREGOR. Yeah, but mine are pretty debilitating.

MARIA. Nothing about you is debilitating. Although I did see your temper once.

GREGOR. You did?

MARIA. We were getting a notary.

GREGOR. Oh yeah! And you were so fascinated by it.

MARIA. By the notary?

GREGOR. No, my temper. In the first book, I described you watching it like you were watching an opera. I thought that was so cool that it didn't scare you. The angrier I got, the more it amused you.

MARIA. Because I know you. I know what's in your heart. And you were standing up for me. It was chivalrous, actually.

GREGOR. It was near the Vons supermarket in Cheviot Hills.

MARIA. The guy wouldn't give me the notary for some reason.

GREGOR. He didn't believe you were you!

MARIA. He was simply determined not to give it to me.

GREGOR. You showed him your license, credit cards, everything. I even showed him your Wikipedia page! Apparently, a lot of ninety-two-year-old ladies are out there trying to swindle notaries.

MARIA. Don't remind me that I met you as an old bag.

GREGOR. Oh be quiet. You may as well have been thirty-two. That's what it felt like. Anyway, he deserved it. He was rude and unreasonable. I saw you get mad once by the way. Once in the three years I took care of you.

MARIA. You did?

GREGOR. You needed help showering one time, and Peter got you a nurse to help you and you got angry.

MARIA. How come you didn't help me?

GREGOR. It would have ruined our relationship.

MARIA. I know it would have, I just wanted to see what you'd say. I miss our poolside chats.

GREGOR. You know, you always saw the light. It's like you were immune to hardship. I mean, even the Holocaust seemed to be something you got through fairly easily.

MARIA. No, darling. Those were terrible times. Breaking up family, country, our way of life, my father passing, all the murders and suicides—it was all hell. I was lucky.

GREGOR. How did you deal with the darkness?

MARIA. I just did, darling. But those were exterior horrors. With you, it's internal.

GREGOR. Yeah.

MARIA. Acknowledge your darkness, darling. Don't fight with it. Your darkness is a part of you, and it's beautiful because it's yours and no one else's. It will fade in time.

GREGOR. I have to go.

MARIA. Where are you going?

GREGOR. To get a haircut and then go to the gym.

MARIA. Don't go giving any old ladies your telephone number. You tell them you're already taken. Okay, my love?

CHAPTER 12

The Chuck Chapters

Part One

Maria's sons, Peter and Jim, and her only daughter, Margie (who now goes by her Hawaiian name "Malia"), are alive and well, living in Tacoma, Washington; Agoura Hills, California; and Kilauea, Hawaii, respectively. They each represent the many different fascinating sides of their mother: Peter, Prince Genial; Jim, Prince Mischievous; and Margie, Princess Charming. Maria's oldest son, Chuck, passed away in 2014. As I sit here laptop-tapping in East Hampton (I'll explain the circumstances around this later), I bring you something I've waited a long time to bring you: The Chuck Chapters. Since a lot needs to be recounted during the twelve months I cared for Chuck after his mother died, I've split the chapters into four parts. These parts are written based on my own experience with him. As far as certain details (his schooling, the kind of car he drove, his time at IBM, etc.), my main sources were Chuck, Margie and Peter.

There are two reasons I wanted to immortalize Chuck in a similar way to how I did it with his mother in the first book: one is so that Maria, who passed away before she got to see me take care of him, could see what that looked like. The second is because Chuck was such a complex and misunderstood character study that I wanted to show you firsthand what I experienced of his heart.

Charles Gustav Altmann was born on August 9, 1940, in a hospital in Fall River, Massachusetts. Brand new parents Maria and Fritz were literally fresh off the boat from England. Eighteen months earlier, around June 1938, Maria and Fritz were on the lam from the Gestapo after escaping house arrest in Vienna. On what would be their final day of house arrest, Maria made up a story that Fritz needed to go to the dentist on account of a painful tooth cavity that left him unable to speak. The trusting parole officer granted the appointment. The newlyweds walked out of the flat, took a taxi to the airport, snuck onto a propeller plane, and were ready to take off to Cologne, Germany where they would eventually reunite with Bernhard at the Holland border.

But before they were high in the sky, there was a moment on that fated runway when it felt like it was all over for them. Maria and Fritz, who minutes ago had strolled out of their Vienna apartment to go to Fritz's would-be dentist appointment, were finally sitting safe in their seats. Suddenly the propellers sputtered out, and four Gestapo marched aboard. Two disappeared into the cockpit, and two skulked up and down the aisles leering at all the passengers. After about twenty minutes of the agony of being certain that she and her husband—a high-profile couple that were now surely being hunted—were going to be arrested and probably killed, the captain got on the loudspeaker and informed everyone that there was bad weather in Munich and they were ready to take off. The Gestapo exited the plane. The doors slammed shut. *Whew.*

Once grounded in Cologne, Maria and Fritz were driven by a Dutch farmer to the German border at Kohlscheid, where they hopped the barbed wire fence and reunited in Holland with Bernhard, who gave them money to fly to Liverpool to start a new life. Bernhard would soon follow them to Liverpool and open a small factory—with the impending war there was a fleeting demand for his textiles. In Liverpool the Altmanns lived comfortably as embryonic Chuck formed in Maria's womb. But the sudden threat of the German Blitz in August 1940 forced Maria and Fritz to abandon Liverpool and board a ship bound for Fall River called the *Britannic*, aka the sister ship of the *Titanic*. The *Britannic* was shot down by a German U-boat on its return to England. (Crowds always gasp when I mention this.)

Maria always loved to say, "Chuck was like a cashmere sweater: made in England and imported to America." (The gasps then inevitably turn to *Chuck*les.)

Chuck died at home in his bed, two weeks before his seventy-fourth birthday, in the early evening hours of July 23, 2014, while the television show *The Bachelor* buzzed in the background. Just three years earlier I had been at the foot his mother's bed, and now, her son's.

In book one, Chuck was prominently featured in many chapters—he lived with his mother and he was hard to miss tooling around the house in his plaid flannel bathrobe from the 1980s with nothing underneath—reminiscent of Gustav Klimt in 1880s' Vienna wearing his smock with, according to Maria, nothing underneath. Maria always joked that Klimt fathered every child in Vienna. There had to be some truth to it.

Speaking of Klimt, Maria loved to share this exchange about her aunt Adele:

"I would ask my mother: 'Did Klimt and Adele have an affair?' And she would snap back, 'How dare you ask such a question? It was an intellectual friendship!'" Then Maria would pause a few moments, turn to me, and say, "So I'm sure they did."

Around the house, Chuck would often get into heated arguments with his mother about how she needed a hearing aid, even though neither of them could hear a word the other was saying. It was guaranteed pure comedy whenever these two were in the same room together.

The following conversation was plucked from one of Chuck and Maria's hearing aid arguments in the kitchen one spring morning in 2010, as documented in the first book:

CHUCK. You look great.

MARIA. What, darling?

CHUCK. *I said you look great!*

MARIA. Not bad for an old bag.

CHUCK. Not bad for what?

MARIA. *I said not bad for an old bag!*

CHUCK. Did you work out with Tina today?

MARIA. Beg pardon?

CHUCK. *Mother, you need a hearing aid!*

MARIA. *I do not need a live-in maid!*

CHUCK. *That's not what I said!*

MARIA. I can hear you. You just mumble.

CHUCK. I don't mumble. *You just can't hear!*

MARIA. Now that I know you mumble, I'll wear my hearing aid.

A beat of silence.

MARIA. I still like you.

CHUCK. You have poor taste.

Boy was Chuck a fascinating dichotomy—one part cashmere sweater and one part tropical storm. But despite this perplexing polarity, I loved him more than he ever knew. He was one of the kindest, sweetest men I ever met, grappling with a monster within that he had next to no control over. Some saw beneath that monster, some refused to. I was one of the ones who always saw the real Chuck … though he never made it easy. We'll get to that crazy year we spent together shortly. But first let's continue with my mother.

CHAPTER 13

Kathryn and Gregor

Part One

Thirty-two years before I met Maria, back when I was zero, I met Kathryn. Some of my earliest memories in life are misbehaving and my mom somehow appearing at some point during it.

When I was around eight, I remember crouching over the edge of a muddy pond at Dana Hall School in Wellesley, Massachusetts, catching bullfrogs. They were slippery and sonorous, and I was awestruck by them—the way they felt like giant bumpy, breathing balloons that could burst open at any moment. I was so enthralled peering around the pond pointing out their muddy heads and imagining rescuing every one of them. I remember catching one, placing it in the bottom of my T-shirt, rolling it up like a burrito, and running back to the dorms where my mom was a counselor. My plan was for no one to know about it at least until I got to my room, but because it wasn't exactly easy hiding a muddy, bloated amphibian who croaks like Barry White, I wasn't exactly inconspicuous. I remember her yelling at me to get it the hell out of the dorm.

Another time, around ten, at a park near the dorms, I found an unopened soft pack of Merit cigarettes. As soon as I picked them up, I felt the most intoxicating adrenaline rush. I slipped them in my pocket and headed home, my heart racing like I was hiding the Hope Diamond.

I got home and sat on my mom's lap, temporarily forgetting about the cigarettes. Noticing the bulge in my pocket, she tapped it, and the plastic crinkled. *The smokes.* She pulled them out. "What are you planning on doing with these, mister?" she asked with questioning brows.

I told her I found them and that I wasn't going to smoke them, which was true. She went and flushed them down the toilet and said something like, "You won't be needing those anymore, Mr. Collins." And I never did.

These were seemingly harmless events, but yet I'm sitting here including them in my book. For me, it was never cigarettes or other physical addictions, even though I tried everything—it was always my independence that I couldn't live without. That was my insurmountable addiction. My biggest fear in life was that I blended in with everyone else. I had no problem making friends, but I usually chose to fly solo— it was the only way I could meet new people, hear new stories, and feel ALIVE. I was always addicted to novelty. I always will be.

My esoteric curiosity has raged since I was little. We had some footage of my brother Christian and me transferred to Vimeo recently, and I watched us as we gallivanted around the house when I was two and Christian was four. I noticed I would occasionally pause with a look of wonder or bewilderment at my surroundings—how strange and interesting it all seemed. At moments, I would find something hilarious and then suddenly become immersed in contemplation. My brother, on the other hand, seemed to have this uninterrupted joviality about everything, nary a moment to think about or absorb anything beyond the task before him. To him, the world didn't seem that strange; it was just kind of what it was supposed to be.

Christian behaved; I rebelled. As teens, when we played tennis as a family at the courts down the street from our house in the Little Rocky Run neighborhood of Clifton, Virginia, I seemed to throw a temper tantrum over every ball I didn't hit perfectly. There were times I'd even storm off the courts in the middle of a point, lock myself in our hot brown station wagon Volvo my mom dubbed The Shit-Mobile, and sit there in a crippling funk until they could drive me home so I could sulk in my room until it was time to go to bed. Christian was the opposite. He didn't overthink anything. If he missed a shot, he'd look to nail the next one. How boring is that?

And as if he needed any more enviable attributes, according to my mom, when he was little, he would befriend the kids who didn't have any friends. If you were an outsider of any kind, you could count on Christian to make you feel like you belonged.

But back to my mom. There were certain things that didn't help along our journey of trying to figure out why we didn't get along. I remember one time I couldn't find my skateboard. I asked her if she had seen it, and she admitted she threw it out. She said she thought it was trash. I couldn't salvage it because the garbage people already took it. It was a Tony Hawk, and it had all the cool stickers on it and everything. I was beside myself.

And it was more fuel for the fire. But how and why did the fire even start? All I knew was that I was secretly praying for instances where I could throw up my arms and go: "See? You see how horrible she is?!"

Though I didn't realize it until much later, part of it must have been the fact that I was scared that if I loved her, then she wouldn't love me back the way I wanted to be loved. It would have been tough love. This is a woman who, as you know, grew up on the South Side slums of Chicago in the 1950s. All she was really doing was living out the tough love—or lack of love—she got as a kid. At any rate, my sensitive soul couldn't take that kind of Chicago love. And as a result of these persistently false perceptions about my mother, I struggled with fully trusting women, as if they all deserved the warped view I had of my mom.

Perhaps my caring for Maria helped erase some of these women issues, although it's interesting to note that Maria didn't care for many women. She found a certain type of woman—what you might refer to as the stuck up, prissy type—to be inauthentic and "put on." (Which reminds me of Oscar Wilde's line: "A man's face is his autobiography; a woman's face is a work of fiction.") She trusted men over women because she felt men were up front about things—what you saw was what you got. That propitious view of men started with her father, Gustav, who she loved with such fervor that even seventy years after his death she would blush at the mere mention of him. Her eyes never sparkled like that when bringing up her mother, although there are some great stories in the first book about her mother and her mother's indomitable sister Luise.

The Collins family dynamic was at best unconventional. Mom was the explosive disciplinarian, and Dad was the intellectual usually off reading a mammoth Winston Churchill book somewhere totally cool with hearing about "what the hell Gregor did now" later or not at all. He cared about me, it wasn't a lack of caring, but it was largely done in passivity that frankly left me curious about a dad who drank and who beat me. *I'd rather feel his hard punches than his pious stares,* was how my secret psyche thought. My dad lives in Geneva now with his wife, who is from the country of Georgia. And I finally have a sister. You met her in the first book during my Golden Trip when she was six. Her name is Annika, and she turns fourteen in 2020. We're total Instagram buddies, but I refuse to make a Tiktok video, I don't care how much she makes me feel guilty about it.

Just like my mother, I've been fiercely autonomous my whole life. As a result, I've been through periods where I'm completely lost about where I'm going. The world makes you feel that way when you think for yourself and go at things alone. It always fascinated me, people like my brother, who always seemed to know exactly where they belonged. Between my dad's unintentional withdrawnness, my mom's role as the enforcer, and Christian's unexplainable indifference, we were somewhat of a ships-passing-in-the-sea type of unit—if we ate dinners together we never really connected on any deep level. We rarely hugged each other. And we didn't even really look like each other. Not exactly what a nuclear family was supposed to be.

I think when you're raised in a colorful-Christmas-sweaters kind of family—that image of everyone looking and dressing exactly the same—you feel a sense of belonging. I never understood how people could see their identities as their families and not as themselves individually. You're in a family, you love each other, but where is it written that you have to be like each other? For some reason it reminds me of the opening line of Tolstoy's *Anna Karenina*: "Happy families are all alike; every unhappy family is unhappy in its own way."

I've always had to fight to feel a part of anything. I've spent much of my adult life seeking institutions, establishments, foundations—anything that would bring me the love and stability I didn't think I got at home. When I met Maria and the Altmanns in 2008, they were the Christmas-sweater family I was afraid to admit I dreamed of, which in a sense brought me closer to my family. I never really had any strong male role models growing up, a scenario I seemed to have adopted from my mother's upbringing. I had no sisters, and the only woman I was raised with—my mom—was one I decided I couldn't stand.

Back to Christian briefly—he and I were only two years apart but had completely different milieus. In high school, I had all black friends, and a black girlfriend named Makeitha. She was darker than the average black girl, so all the white kids who were part of the whole "collective-thinking system" would look at me like I was some alien from another planet. I don't know why, but I found black girls more exciting than white girls. Christian's friends used to see me swaggering down the hallways in my baggy jeans below the waste, sporting double-hoop earrings with my pink pager attached to my belt, a black girl hanging on my arm, and must have shook their heads and thought: "There goes Christian's brother." People could never really figure me out; they didn't know how to define me. And that didn't sit well with those inside a system that they didn't even know they were in.

I had some major street cred because of my basketball skills. I played high school ball, but it was on the courts after school for pickup games when I became known as the white Michael Jordan because of my tongue-wagging moves. Hanging out with my basketball cronies led me to befriend a few unsavory characters, and we got into trouble a lot.

Once we had a contest: whoever could steal the biggest item from a grocery store without getting caught would win. This guy Tremain managed to steal a whole turkey. He just walked out with it without even trying to hide it. He never got caught, so he won. I don't remember if he returned the turkey. I wouldn't bet on it.

Another time about a dozen of us put our money together to buy two hundred dollars' worth of groceries we used to decimate the house of a guy we hated at school—his name was Peter Barron. We splattered yogurt on the windows, poured motor oil all over the flower beds, squeezed tubes of mustard into the pool, and wrote "Fuck You, Peter" in shaving cream on his front lawn. We were so proud of what we accomplished.

But we got caught red-handed. Peter's parents opened an investigation and found grocery store footage of us buying all the supplies. They didn't press charges, but we had to go to their house— the house we ruined with groceries just two nights before—and apologize to Peter and his parents. It was emotional and tearful and humiliating for us to have to face that music. Imagine how it felt for Peter and his family.

One night during my junior year of high school my friend Will Burch, his girlfriend Hyacinth, and I were bored and decided pulling out stop signs would spruce things up. We started in my neighborhood, down the street from my house. While Hyacinth waited in the car, Will and I pulled out two signs before being caught red-handed—pun intended—by a police officer sitting in his unmarked car a few feet away. He got out and walked right up to us as we both stood frozen, hugging the giant pole. It was right out of a Hallmark Channel movie.

"What were you gentlemen thinking of doing with that stop sign?"

"Oh, this? We were just making sure it was in there good. Yep, it's in there. See ya."

Apparently, my neighbor Glen called the cops on us. When Will and I were standing in court answering to our crime, I saw Glen sitting in the court pews. I was wondering what he was doing there—turns out he was wondering the same thing about me. He leaned over in the pews and asked why I was there. I told him I was caught pulling out a stop sign. Glen's face sunk into his palms. He had just realized that he had called the cops on *me*; all he saw was two dark figures and picked up the phone. He was so embarrassed and apologetic, but c'mon, we deserved it. We were lucky we didn't cause a fatality.

Will and I went to the slammer for two days. A guy I met in our cell asked what we were in for, and I said pulling out street signs. "Nah, man," he said, "keep that stupid ass shit to yourself." He was in for a much cooler crime: B&E (breaking and entering).

That whole jail debacle was the last straw. When I went off to college, I became something resembling an upstanding citizen—I made the golf team (I played all four years in high school, too), eventually studied the entertainment business, and upon graduating from Florida State drove out to Los Angeles to work in reality television, then become an actor, and then stumble into a kitchen in Cheviot Hills to meet "some ninety-two-year-old lady needing a caregiver."

Through all these life events, though, my relationship with my mother remained an open wound. Why couldn't we just get along? There were things I liked about her. She was strong. She was charismatic. She made big, delicious salads for me after school when all the other kids would mostly get McDonalds. I wanted to find a woman who was all of these things, but not one who acted like her in all the other ways I didn't like.

Once in 2001 during a meeting with my boss Harley Tat while working on a reality television show called *Blind Date*, he gazed out the window and said, "You know, Gregor, life is like the stock market—it has its ups and downs, but in the end … It's always up." That *always up* part stuck with me. Even though he ended up being a real jerk, it was very Maria Altmann of him to say.

And so it goes, dear reader, that after decades of ups and downs with my mother, there's an *always up* ending coming down the pike. But let's first dive head first into the one and only Charles Gustav Altmann.

CHAPTER 14

The Chuck Chapters

Part Two

Chuck was born to be wild—and the wild began early.

While according to a few Google clicks it's fairly common for a baby in utero to have the umbilical cord inadvertently wrapped around his or her neck, it isn't as common for the cord to be tangled around the entire body, as it was with newborn Chuck. So before little Charlie could be held and hugged by his exhausted mother, a team of doctors and nurses had to perform an impromptu operation to untangle his body from the cord. It was successful.

But it set a tone.

A few days after the umbilical debacle, this happened, as relayed to me by Maria in the first book:

> The story of the day was a wild one about a Saturday night in Fall River, Massachusetts, in late November, 1940. A few weeks earlier Chuck had made his way out of his mother's womb. They were at home, amidst a huge blizzard. "I looked out onto the street and the cars looked like giant white potatoes," remembered Maria.
>
> Chuck suddenly started vomiting, and it didn't let up. "After a while there was nothing left for him to throw up." Maria dialed the doctor at his home, and calmly explained what was happening. The doctor reassured her everything would be okay and that he'd visit them first thing Monday morning. "He later told me that while I was on the phone

with him he was already putting on his snow boots and hat, and looking for his car keys."

The doctor made it to the house within the hour. The vomiting had subsided, and all was back to normal. Then Maria asked me, "Do you know what the doctor's name was?" I shook my head. "Dr. Blood," she responded earnestly. I verified it with Chuck.

The drama continued.

When Chuck was two Maria took him with her to a local strip mall in Fall River. While walking through a department store, he suddenly vanished. She scoured the store, soliciting employees to help with the search. They finally found him in the front display window, having climbed atop a high shelf, in danger of tumbling off any moment. When Maria pulled him down, she no doubt attributed his recalcitrance to those terrible twos. Little did she know, it would last into his seventies.

For the first few years of Chuck's life, much of his mother's energy was spent putting out fires that he started. Maria had survived the Holocaust, had lost countless friends and family members to execution and suicide, and in her eighties had fought an entire nation for nearly a decade to recover her uncle Ferdinand's Klimt paintings, but as anyone who knew her would tell you, handling her oldest son over the course of her life was probably her most daunting undertaking. You could make a legitimate case that it wasn't the fight to get those paintings back that was her biggest accomplishment in life; it was keeping her family sane in the midst of the monsoon that could be Chuck.

But despite catching her fair share of criticism for it, Maria remained his fiercest supporter until the very end. It seems fitting that they passed away so close to each other, Chuck only two years after his mother. You could say he died of a broken heart.

Despite Chuck's volcanic temper and his refusal to do anything conventionally, I had a soft spot for him. It wasn't just that he was the son of a mother who herself was impossible not to love. There wasn't any loving by association on my part. There were two things about Chuck that made me love him: first, he had a kind heart that I pointed out often and for which I got a lot of pushback from people who suffered by him. And second, I empathized with him.

My mother told me something once in 2018 during a heated argument—that when I was a kid I had to do everything my own way, no matter what it was. If someone did something perfectly efficiently right in front of me, I had to go off and do it the harder way just so I could say I did it my own way. They did a poll on Reddit once about which side of the shower most people step out of, the far side or the showerhead side. The majority of people said they got out on the far side. I remember I was at the apartment of a girl I was dating in 2018 and got out of the shower on the showerhead side. She was fascinated by that and brought up the aforementioned Reddit poll. So for better or for worse, my soft spot for Chuck was because we were both born nonconformists. The world didn't make sense to Chuck and me because Chuck and me didn't make sense to the world.

There was such a sweetness in Chuck, but—and even Maria would admit to this, in much flowerier language—you also often wanted to throw him off a moving train. On paper you would almost think he was engaging in some kind of performance art. But no, Chuck in person was 100 percent himself every second of every day.

Chuck's early teens were spent at Catholic school, when the school's headmaster, Mother Mary, asked Maria to remove Chuck from the school immediately. Margie told me this story, and after I texted her asking her why, she never responded. I could only imagine it had something to do with Chuck's proclivity for yelling for no apparent reason. This expulsion led to him being sent to military school in the Valley—his father, Fritz's, idea.

While Fritz was the embodiment of Captain von Trapp from the movie *The Sound of Music*—implementing high discipline and stringent rules—Maria was Maria von Trapp—all about acceptance and love. While Fritz viewed Chuck as impossible, Maria viewed him as … challenging. It was glass half empty/glass half full parenting in its purest form. Chuck left military school despising it, and his mother was the one who picked him up promising he would never return. Chuck's high school years were spent at Beverly Hills High, and then Santa Monica City College. He graduated from the University of Southern California School of Engineering in 1962.

Since connecting with others was always a challenge, Chuck found comfort in numbers and airplanes. If he wasn't working on computer code, he was at the Santa Monica airport, sitting in the parking lot in his 1956 black-and-white Chevy Bel Air, watching takeoffs and landings from sunup to sundown. In 1968, at age twenty-six, Chuck consummated his love of numbers by landing a job at IBM as an engineer, where he would work gainfully for thirty years. Also in 1968, he married his first wife, Sheila, with whom he had two sons, Ken and Phil. Today, Ken works at a major social media company, and Phil works as an entertainment attorney.

Chuck retired from IBM in 1996 and moved to Danalda Drive to live with his mother, where I would meet them both twelve years later. At Danalda, he would stay for the next fifteen years, until Maria's death in 2011. As you might recall from the first book, Chuck vowed he would not move out of his mother's house until she died, a promise he stuck to firmly until the end. Even after he remarried in 2008, he insisted on sleeping at his mother's while his new wife slept alone at their new house.

Turns out Chuck's sleepover stubbornness paid off. In late 2010, two months before Maria died—on a weekend I was not at the house— Maria tripped on a hairbrush on the floor of her bathroom. After hearing her wails, Chuck, with another caregiver, Tom (the guy who got me the job in 2008), ran from his room down the hallway to lift her off the floor. I had never seen Chuck run; I had never heard of Chuck running; in fact, I didn't even know Chuck could run. Chuck didn't run for anybody. But Chuck ran for his mother.

In 2006, Chuck met his second wife, Donna. Here's an excerpt about their meeting from the first book:

> On one of his ambles through the kitchen, Chuck tells us he's off to his girlfriend Donna's house in Huntington Beach. They met on Match.com. He told me: "I wrote in my profile that I wanted a woman within ten miles and no pets, and I end up with a woman 45 miles away with 8 pets. That's internet dating for you.

He had another story he loved to tell about Donna: "I said to my therapist once: There's something I don't like about her. I kept saying that to him over and over until one session he said to me: 'Let me ask you something—do you think there's something about *you* that *she* doesn't like?' That changed everything for me. I married her after that!"

It was a minor miracle to most people who knew Chuck: he had met someone who could actually tolerate him for an extended period of time. In 2008, a few weeks after I started caring for Maria, Chuck married Donna in the backyard of their new home on Fairburn Avenue in Los Angeles. A few weeks later, Chuck's younger brother Peter married a Donna in Seattle, and to make it even more confusing, both Donnas shared the middle name Marie. How would we tell the difference between the two Donna-Maries? We called Chuck's Donna *LaDonna*, for Los Angeles Donna, and Peter's Donna *SeaDonna*, for Seattle Donna.

During the spring of 2013, two years after Maria's passing, I moved in with Chuck and Donna on Fairburn Avenue. This was completely unplanned. As far as I was concerned, my thirty-seven months with Maria was my first and last caregiving job. I had won the caregiving lottery, and I didn't even buy a ticket. It was time to get back to hanging out with young people and focusing solely on my career in the arts, whatever that was going to be. But Chuck needed someone who wasn't a blood family member who could see things from a different perspective.

Aside from being at the apex of his incorrigibility, Chuck, seventy-two at the time, was in a steep decline in health and mobility, which made his irascibility even more intense than usual. While Margie makes clear that Chuck was "very gentle with me and guided me through many decisions in my teens," Peter and Jim have said in the past in no uncertain terms that they spent their lives terrorized by their big brother's temper. Either way, I was there to provide relief to anyone who needed it. My door was always open, and my phone was always on.

Of prime concern was Chuck's ailing back. After decades of excruciating pain, at age sixty-nine, he had back surgery. Unfortunately, it wasn't entirely successful. He continued to have aches and spasms, a cruel fate for a man who was born explosive enough. During my three years with his mother, Chuck's lower back was almost always preventing him from being able to enjoy standing for any reasonable length of time. The funniest and saddest thing in the world was seeing a ninety-two-year-old mother ask her seventy-two-year-old son if he needed a chair. His back had gotten to the point where, if he had walked or been standing for sixty seconds and couldn't find somewhere to sit, it wasn't, "Hey, could you try and find me a chair please?" it was *"Where the fuck is a goddamned chair, goddamn it!"* Chuck's impassioned pursuit of chairs and ledges around Beverly Hills became our primary mission when we left the house. I could never blame him.

What I *could* blame him for was his impetuous temper—but I was half at fault, because I faced that temper with a lack of patience. When we clashed, it was temper versus no-patience: a sonic boom heard throughout all of Los Angeles. At the end of the day, though, I had cared for his mother, and that was the final say in every one of our arguments. For example, if I closed his car door the slightest bit harder than usual, he would go from zero to sixty in less than a second. Then, when the verbal bombing subsided, we'd sit back in his luxurious Lexus, share a Maria story, and everything would calm down. If I had a dollar for every loving shoulder-rub Chuck gave me after sharing stories about his mother, I'd be worth as much as his mother was.

Chuck inherited many of Maria's best qualities. In many ways, they were cut from the same cloth. Her playful wit, her captivating stories, and her kindheartedness all filtered straight into Chuck's bloodstream, and on a good day, he was the walking embodiment of everything that was amazing in her. As impossible as Chuck could be, if he was in the right chair in the right mood with the right people, he could be as smooth as Cary Grant and as warm as Michelle Obama.

But he also inherited a quality that was a major contributor to his untimely death. And though Maria didn't have many bad qualities, this one quality that Chuck inherited from her was a pretty lethal one: an aversion to exercise.

CHAPTER 15

Kathryn and Gregor

Part Two

In Spring 2019, my mother was descending the flight of stairs in her apartment complex in a rush to a meeting at her office across the street when she caught a heel on the last stair and tumbled onto the hard marble floor. She didn't break anything or fall anywhere near her head, thank goodness, but she bruised her hip and shoulder pretty badly to the point where she couldn't lift her arms above her head. When I heard about the fall in New York, I took the earliest Amtrak I could to Virginia. This was unfamiliar territory. My mom was always sprite and active. At seventy-two, she looked and acted like she was in her fifties.

Because we were never a touchy-feely family, I wasn't accustomed to showing physical affection to her. Even though caring for Maria left me open to care more for others, my mother and I were still standoffish, even during times we were enjoying each other's company. But the situation at hand demanded my being out of my comfort zone in a physical way. She needed help with a lot of things. Since she couldn't raise her arms, I helped her comb and curl her hair. And she had dropped her shampoo in the shower a couple days earlier and couldn't pick it up—I picked it up. They were small things, but they were *monumental* things for our relationship.

Somehow, the simple act of helping her with these menial tasks seemed to instantaneously dismantle decades of struggle. It was like we were in traffic our entire lives, and then, suddenly the road opened up—and all those years sitting in traffic were completely erased from our memories. I had always loved her, I just didn't know how to show it. As a result of that fall and those depressing months for her that followed, I had an opportunity to show my love in a conspicuous way. Though we would inevitably have our head-butting moments and it would never be perfect, I could always point to my mom's recovery months as a time when we rose to a new level in our kinship.

We continue to grow. She goes out of her way more to show me she understands me. One time she felt really depressed for no reason. She called me. "I never get like this, Gregor, I mean depression is not in my vocabulary, but I want to tell you that now I know what you go through when you say you're depressed. It must be terrible." Another time, she said to me: "When you are *you*, Gregor, you light up the world." I'm working on being *me* much more.

One time I was visiting her in Reston and I went to throw a piece of paper out. Naturally, I crumpled it up and threw it in the trash. She laughed. "Why do you crumple? Just fold it like this. It takes up less space." I told her it's much more fun to crumple. The crumple/ fold thing is the perfect metaphor for us. Mom folds, I crumple. She's pragmatic, I'm impulsive.

I get a lot of my artistic sense from her. We're both aesthetes. We've always seen eye to eye on art and design. Rising above her uncouth beginnings, she developed a sophisticated sense of style that rubbed off on me. We bond over home design: minimal, modern, crisp whites, stone greys, bursts of colors emanating from paintings and carpets. And things like paper towels in the kitchen. I would never leave rolls out in the open. The sight of it makes me cringe. They get stuffed in a cupboard. She's the same. And dishrags. You would never walk into our homes and find a dishrag draped through the refrigerator door handle. That would be tacky. Whenever I visit her we always take the Metro in to the National Gallery of Art. At this point we know pretty much every painting and sculpture they own. And when it comes to art movements, our sweet spot is from about 1890 to 1920. From Van gogh/Cezanne to Matisse/Picasso, and everything in between.

One thing that has become clear is that Mom and I cannot afford to not love and support each other anymore. We are stuck together like conjoined twins, and how we treat ourselves directly and immediately affects how we treat each other. Somebody told me once that sons who have trouble finding a woman often have something in common: a strong mother. I don't know if that applies to us, but it fills me with gratitude to think that if she wasn't this strong woman she would never have escaped her past and blessed me with the gift of life—and a damn good one at that.

Before I left Reston the last time I visited my mom, I grabbed my bag and walked around to her side of the car:

"Just know that you are loved," I told her. It just tumbled out. I had never said that to her before—ever—in my life.

CHAPTER 16

Breather

Screech! Because we've covered a lot in an intense way—and the chapter after this one amps it up to another level—I'd like for us to take a breather here, not to have to invest too much of our mental energy before we suit up again for Chapter 17.

———◆———

Even though I was always fairly certain I was doing a good job caring for their mother, once in a while I'd get affirmations from the kids that were deeply felt. In the spring of 2019, after I told Margie I was working on the sequel to the first book, she texted me this story. I vaguely remember her telling me about it after it happened, but it now holds much more meaning all these years later.

> Did I ever tell you the story of Mom at age 91, dressed in her robe at 8:30 in the morning, sitting on the kitchen table, waiting for you to arrive? I had flown in from Hawaii the night before & arrived at midnight. The monitor in the kitchen woke me up with her meandering and I went in sleepily. She greeted me sweetly & surprised and when I asked her, "Why are you up so early?" She replied, "I am waiting for Gregor." I replied, "I gave him the day off so I thought we could spend some time together." Her reply, "How dare you do that without asking me!" That is the day I knew how much she cared for you.

Margie also reminded me of another story—how two weeks into the job I had set fire to the backyard trash bin after dumping hot coals into it after a barbecue. I never put it in the first book because when I started writing it I thought there might be a chance I would publish while Maria was still alive, and I didn't want her to know that the week the house smelled like burnt plastic was because of me.

Anyway, how it transpired was, after Maria had gone to take a nap and I plunked down on the den couch to watch television, I started to smell smoke, ran out of the room and around the side of the house, and was lucky to discover the flames early enough to douse it with a bucket of water. It ended up burning a few panels on the side of the house and obliterated the air conditioner. We lived in a sauna for a few days until the new AC arrived. I'm forever grateful the kids always kept that secret for me.

———— • ————

Maria loved animals, especially rabbits. Just like Chicago dogs were to my mother, rabbits held sentimentality. She had them as pets throughout her childhood. Reminiscing about those thriving pre-Hitler days in Vienna was one of Maria's favorite pastimes. After eighty years the memories must have bounced around in her head like a fantasy from a distant dream.

"If you were an animal, what animal would you be?" I asked her once during a poolside chat.

She paused to think.

"Not a rabbit?" I asked.

"I'm not cute enough to be a rabbit," she replied. "I'd be a panther."

"What kind of panther?" I asked.

"Just a regular old panther, My Love."

My answer is unoriginal, I suppose: I'd be a bird. But the real question is, what kind of bird would you be? I think it depends on your preference in cars. You might be a finch, darting around like a Porsche on a racetrack. You might be an eagle, soaring around like a Rolls-Royce on Rodeo Drive. You might be a pigeon, jerking around like an old pickup truck on a bumpy road.

You might even be an ostrich—only the one car you couldn't be would be a flying car.

CHAPTER 17

Halfway to Life

I wrote this chapter in the fall of 2018 during a stretch of darkness. I wanted to set some things straight about the world I thought needed to be set straight. I included it in the book because I wanted to imagine how Maria would have reacted to sides of me she never knew were there. I kept most of this kind of moroseness hidden from her, not for fear of her judging me, because she never judged anyone, but because it would have taken away from the cheerful tone we always fostered.

One of Maria's best qualities was that she never spent time casting aspersions on people. In fact, she saw bad people less as being bad and more as a challenge to disarm, and if she couldn't disarm them, she winked and moved on jovially. The only types of people who seemed to get under her skin were boring people—people with nothing interesting to say. They bewildered her to no end. They were almost worse to her than bad people because at least bad people had a sense of danger to them, and that was interesting to her. In the terminally curious mind of Maria, if you were charming and charismatic, your malfeasances took a temporary back seat—she was only human. Remember, though, Maria grew up a Bloch-Bauer, which was like growing up a Rockefeller, so she was accustomed to balls and galas and all the charismatic company that came with high society.

Maria brought me tranquility during times of tumult with her go-to solution to life's problems: "Everything will be okay, my love." I truly believed her whenever she said it. Though her easygoing wisdom often felt frustratingly simplistic, especially to an over-thinker like me who makes mountains out of molehills, by the end of this chapter, simplicity is exactly what I stumble on.

———————•————————

To what depths a person feels reveals how difficult that person's life will be. The deeper you feel, the tougher your life. There are ways to soften the blows through family or spirituality but by and large, if you feel deeply, you feel isolated, and you have to work extra hard if you want to fit in. I've always been a deep feeler. So when Goethe wrote, "The soul that sees beauty may sometimes walk alone," he was talking about people like me.

If you feel … you feel pain. You feel joy too, but pain is what defines your life. That the world sometimes feels like a strange and lonely place is a feeling reserved exclusively for owners of kind hearts. No one with an unkind heart ever felt that the world was a strange or lonely place, on account of being too busy contaminating it. But because I'm willing to be optimistic and say that every bad human began as a good human, at one time in the early years, when he or she was pure in heart, that person surely felt the world strange and lonely and longed for it to someday feel sensible and welcoming.

These eleven simple words by A. E. Housman in 1901: "I, a stranger and afraid, in a world I never made," have always made me *feel* a certain way about our increasingly outer-obsessed world.

There was a poll done in 2019 by the research firm Morning Consult that found that Generation Z considers fame and fortune even more important to their lives than millennials do. Twelve percent of Gen Zers say that fame is very important to them, compared to just 7 percent of millennials. We're headed in the wrong direction.

One of the problems in this increasingly outer world is that the marketing powers that be propagate the idea that more is better. The more options you have, the better your life will be; you've got to keep gathering things, or you'll miss out. In fact, the psyche works in the exact opposite way: The fewer options you have, the more fulfilling the option you choose will be. Conversely, the more options you have, the more having less has you thinking you have nothing at all. And most of us buy into it all because we see with our eyes and not our hearts.

We live in a world where complexity and nuance aren't rewarded like they used to be, which means that the genius of many of our bygone thinkers would have been completely misunderstood in today's world. Trump would have belittled them on Twitter. "Did everyone here what blockhead Mark Twain just said? SAD!" And, of course, it would have gotten a gazillion retweets.

We live in a world where we've stopped listening to ourselves. And because we've stopped listening to ourselves, we can't hear others. And in lieu of hearing others, we hear our dings on our phones. And they soothe us, each ding leading us further and further away from having to face our true nature. This makes for a shallow life. Superficial things bring superficial satisfaction.

I was on an Amtrak to DC the other day to visit my mom in Reston, Virginia, and I sat behind two girls who, for the majority of the three-hour ride, almost never glimpsed at the passing scenery. Instead, they were buried in their phones posting Instagram photos—and, at times, not even new ones. They would go back to old photos they already posted and change the image filter to make them look more physically appealing. Not that I was watching them like a hawk or anything or had a perfect angle to see it all unfold. The only conversations they had with each other were about conversations they were having with commenters on their social media channels. But in the end, I lost because I was the one who was miserable.

I read this about the internet *on* the internet recently and thought it was very true: "Fifteen years ago, the internet was an escape from the real world. Today, the real world is an escape from the internet." I worry about my thirteen-year-old sister, Annika. She's outgoing, entertaining, and sharp, and I think she's not helping her mental growth by being so reliant on electronic devices. But she's being a normal kid these days. I worry that all these tweens born after smartphones won't ever have any practicable potential to truly know themselves.

Maybe I didn't hate those girls on the Amtrak; maybe I hated their smartphones; maybe I hated Steve Jobs. There is nothing more glaringly destroying what's left of humanity than the entire planet locked in that downward Quasimodo position, right? That human banana walking down the street on the phone like a digital zombie. You'd think knowing we're gonna die someday would cause us to at least look up from our phones once in a while.

Things don't make sense in a world of black and white. We're told to be tough yet open. If you're just tough, you survive, but you don't truly live. If you're just open, you're living, but you may not survive. We're told to be goal-oriented, yet if we're obsessed with goals we miss out on the present moment. How should we live? Who in this brave new world can maintain a proper balance?

If you're an interesting person, you live an interesting life, a boring person a boring life, but everything, even good things, comes with a caveat—the interesting life is the tougher life, the boring life, the easier life. So what should you choose? And is it even a choice? Life can be a magical and miserable thing because you have to be yourself and think for yourself, yet if you don't blend in, people ostracize you. How do you be yourself and blend in at the same time? It's an imperfect science. What's beautiful about life is that it's a lens, and that lens is different for every person who looks through it. I happen to have a very complicated lens that I daily fight to simplify. Maria kept it simple for me, and because of that, the three years with her were probably the most mentally productive of my life.

I recently hit forty. No, I'm not in a midlife crisis. After I tell people my age, they love to go: "Midlife crisis, eh?" Again, no, for the same reason I don't say to someone's grandma after she forgets something: "Dementia, eh?" You know, because I can think for myself.

It's to be expected in a world of sheep. The reality is that humans are a species who follow the majority. The mob mentality is actually biological. Scientists have done studies showing that only 5 percent of a crowd can influence the direction of the other 95 percent. The 95 percent follow without even realizing who or what they're following. Yet the cruelness of it is, that same 95 percent (the girls on the Amtrak) are the ones who are having the best time. Ignorance will always be bliss.

As he often does, Mark Twain comes to mind here: "Don't let schooling interfere with your education." Sheep, you see, learn everything from school, leaders learn everything from life experience. The Indian mystic Sadhguru, one of my YouTube obsessions, said in a discussion with the neuroscientist David Eagleman: "I am uneducated. Proudly." To Sadhguru, being uneducated is an achievement, because it means he hasn't allowed himself to identify with anything but his own being. "The moment you identify with anything," he explains, "your body, your family, your community, your nation, humanity … you are limited."

Some of today's woke kids are fighting this mob mentality on social media. The young poet Rune Lazuli, who shot to fame recently when Lady Gaga started retweeting her instagram memes, writes in one meme: "We spend lifetimes searching endless fields for a cave of gold that is hidden in our hearts." It's been said many different ways throughout history, but the point is, someone who isn't even 21 years old is posting that on Instagram. That's a step in the right direction.

Barring extenuating circumstances, it's our choice if we live in joy or in misery. I'm smart. I have above average intelligence. But let's be honest. The true curse on a person is above average intelligence. Not that Ernest Hemingway is the picture of all truth, but he said, "Happiness in intelligent people is the rarest thing that I know." And the desire for change is something only intelligent people know about. All intelligent people don't necessarily want to change, but unintelligent people don't know what change is.

How can I ever be at peace when I know stuff? If you can keep your blissful ignorance, keep it, because once you have that first taste of truth—and you dive deeper and deeper into that truth—you are sitting in a boat that has just sprung a leak. The moment you start opening books and watching documentaries and ending up in that weird part of YouTube, you start to know things you can never un-know—things that threaten your whole belief system.

Like the *big rip*. At some point in the future, the universe will stretch to the point that it will literally rip apart at the seams, down to the tiniest molecule. Our very fabric of existence will be dismembered. Here's another doozy—the *local group*, the term for our galaxy? To give you an idea of how big our galaxy is, it's three hundred million light years across, and our local group is just one of millions of galaxies. Eventually, our galaxy will drift so far away from all the other galaxies that the astronomers of the day will look out and see total blackness everywhere. They'll think there's nothing else in existence but the spinning rock-ball they're riding headed nowhere. Do you see how the more you know, the less favors you're doing for yourself? Too much attention is placed on knowing, anyway. To un-know, to strip off all the crap you've been told your whole life, now that is the only true path to inner peace. I didn't fully absorb this until I hit my 40's.

But even knowing that I need to un-know, my questions still don't stop.

Do I believe in God, or *am* I god? Am I a Christian or a Buddhist? A liberal or a conservative? Is God somebody else who has infinite power, and I, the seeker, am feeble? Or are I and God *one* in both the inner and the outer life? How can you ever be sure who you are or what you want? Isn't it impossible for the godhead to be the subject of its own knowledge? Isn't it impossible for a knife to be able to cut itself? Why is it that I simply must know the full truth in order to put one foot in front of the other? Why can't I just peel the potato instead of wondering why the hell I'm peeling it? What the hell do I want? Or what the hell do I think I'll get if I ask for what I truly want?

I'm meditating more these days to help fight my racing mind. But I find it nearly impossible to be consistent. *Practice, practice.*

In the Far East—we'll take India and Japan, for example—the spiritual goal is to be desireless and purposeless. But in the Western world, we desire stuff. If we don't feel a purpose, we feel worthless. I'm caught somewhere in between.

I'm unclear about a lot of things. They say Karma is a bitch, but what about at the end of a life? How do I know bad humans go to a bad place when they die? Maybe they don't. Maybe Maria is in hell, and Hitler is in heaven. Maybe it doesn't matter what you did or what you said on Earth. Good people do bad things; bad people do good things; nature both kills and nurtures. Life is a paradox, one moment having infinite possibilities and, the next, infinite nothingness. So if this is how random life is, how capricious it can be, how do we know it won't pull another fast one on us when we die?

Dear reader, I don't think you can ever be completely clear about where you're going … you just get more comfortable being unclear. You know what they say—trust those who seek the truth, and don't trust those who say they've found it. Charles Bukowski's epic poem "Genius of the Crowd" comes to mind here: "Beware the preachers … beware the knowers."

There are a lot of problems with the world; extremes, in my opinion, being a significant one. Extremes are lethal, never benign. Extreme liberalism is just as bad as extreme conservatism; alpha males (Donald Trump) are just as bad as alpha females (Kim Kardashian); under-eating is just as bad as overeating. *Balance is peace.* It's one of the reasons why Bernie Sanders and Elizabeth Warren will never win an election. Biden, the centrist—at least centrist in comparison to Sanders and Warren—is in my eyes the only Democrat who has a shot against Trump in 2020.

I saw a movie once called *Jackie* starring Natalie Portman, and there's a scene with Jackie and a priest, played by John Hurt, where the priest says to Jackie: "There comes a time in man's search for meaning when he realizes he has no answers and that he must stop searching."

Do we find peace simply by not searching for it? It's a promising start. The best times in my life are when I'm not searching for anything. I'm living in the moment in self-love and self-acceptance like I was in Australia. I've noticed that at times in my life I've been too afraid to be my true self because I don't have what I want, and only after deep contemplation do I realize that I don't have what I want because I'm too afraid to be my true self.

Let's not forget that we're living in a miracle. I mean, the simple fact is that if you get hurt, you heal. If you fall off your bike and skin your knee, a week later you have a brand-new knee. Whatever force created us insisted, "They have to be self-healing."

Existence is a miracle! That's the only truth! Take language—the way we absorb things without ever learning how to do it. How could we as human beings, the light of the Earth, the jewels of existence, not be the center of the universe? Each one of us. I mean, why would we be created such incredibly sensitive, incomprehensibly complex mechanisms of hope and joy and genius and love if our imaginations didn't hold the master key to everything?

The reality is, there is a ball of fire up there in the sky. That stays hot. That formed long before humans ever needed it. It was there billions of years before humans showed up, and just in case something called *humans* ever came down the pike one day, it was far enough away from these humans to not burn them to death. And that perfectly crafted sun gives them nice tans so they can appear attractive to others and reproduce and keep humanity going.

Why can't we consistently wake up to this magical existence? To think, we are presented with a world of vast adventures and endless possibility yet we go to one school, get one job, work in one building, drive one way home, have one romantic partner, and choose our tiny little crawlspace to inhabit until we die. The worlds we miss out on!

Living correctly is the opposite of catching a fly. To catch a fly, you have to slap down where the fly is *going* to go, not where it actually is. But in life, you need to go where it *is*, not where it's *going* to go. Norman Lear, who at age ninety-seven was the oldest person to win an Emmy in 2019, said after winning, "I don't think about my life a lot. I like getting up in the morning."

The present moment.

CHAPTER 18

Sydney

In the summer of 2017, Diane Symonds, a perfect stranger, was at London Heathrow airport waiting for her flight to Mykonos, just finishing up a book she had downloaded on her Kindle called *The Accidental Caregiver*. She was, as she later told me, so moved by it that she did something she had never done before: reached out to the author. Before she boarded the flight, she logged onto Facebook, found a profile resembling me, and without thinking it would result in a reply, sent me the following note. I've included the string of correspondences that led up to the speaking tour.

July 20, 2017

Hi Gregor, not sure if you will get this message but felt like reaching out and saying hi. I have just finished reading your heartfelt book and wanted to say thank you for sharing such an incredible journey and giving us a glimpse into the beautiful relationship you shared with Maria.

July 21, 2017

Diane! Thank you so much for this note, it was a beautiful thing to get before I go to bed early :) I see you live in Australia … cheers from New York!! (just curious how you found out about the book?)

July 21, 2017

Hi, yes I live in Sydney. Born in New York. Dad's a Brooklyn boy and mum was born in Tel Aviv. I'm travelling at the moment in London on my trip to Mykonos and have my Kindle with me. I had seen Woman in Gold which I loved and when I was searching for a book to download yours came up. I had just finished reading the Zoo Keepers Wife which is also brilliant.

July 21, 2017

Very cool - I've only seen the movie. Safe travels to you. Thanks again.

It was left at that, until ...

September 7, 2017

Hi Gregor, how are you? Wanted to chat about the possibility of coming to Sydney as a guest speaker for our Sponsor a Child function next May. It's a charity that raises money for women and children in Israel called WIZO. Each year we host a lunch with a guest speaker and I thought of you. I think your beautiful story would appeal to our donors. Is this something that you do? If you think this is something you might be interested in please let me know. Thanks.

After I finished all my engagements in Melbourne, it was on to Sydney, where, before all six of my events, Di—who during the tour was promoted to president of WIZO Sydney—was up there explaining how we met.

As an aside, all the while I was corresponding with Diane on Facebook in 2017, I was in Amsterdam for the first time. An extremely wealthy woman I had met in 2016 had hired me to talk her drug-addicted son, who lived in Amsterdam and whom I had never met before, into moving to New York to get cleaned up and be closer to his mother. She had failed so many times that I seemed to be her last hope. This wasn't the plot of a movie I had seen—it actually happened. And by the way, her son ended up moving to New York soon after our meeting.

Ah, Sydney, Australia—the hilliness of San Francisco and the beach life of Los Angeles, although, when it came to the LA comparison, I found Sydney's beaches more stunning, the people kinder and more approachable, and the air (obviously) crisper and cleaner. But what made Oz unique is what also made it a royal bummer: that it was so far from everything. This made it safe, clean—a kind of pacifistic paradise—but it was a twenty-one-hour flight from pretty much anywhere in the Americas or Europe. Most people I told that I was headed to Australia, said, "I've always wanted to go, but it's too far!"

In Sydney I spoke at everything from a private home on Bondi Beach for twenty-five people to a Jewish children's daycare for fifty, to a synagogue for seventy-five, to a brunch on the Sydney Harbor—the main keynote talk—for 120.

Back in Melbourne, Lorna, the executive director of WIZO Sydney, texted me: "Have they told you where you're staying when you arrive in Sydney?" All I knew was that it was near the most famous beach in Australia, Bondi Beach. When I got to Bondi, it was not only near the beach, it was practically *on* it. The place in which I was staying belonged to a film producer named Jonathan Shteinman who was kind enough to lend me his apartment. This was clearly not like living in New York in my dingy Midtown prison cell wedged into the concrete jungle like rows of crowded teeth.

The "Love, Maria" events felt as impactful as the ones that came before. I assumed after I'd bawled in Melbourne, though, I'd be able to keep it together in Sydney, and as always, I did up until the moment I had to speak. But every single time I opened up my mouth, whether for twenty people or two hundred, it was like I was watching the movie *Terms of Endearment* for the fortieth time—it was impossible not to choke back tears. At least I was consistent. And my consistency was proof that no one who attended any of these events could ever say my love for that woman wasn't genuine—after all, when I took the caregiving job in 2008, I had no idea who Maria was other than she was ninety-two and from Austria. I fell for her before knowing anything about her childhood or the Klimt paintings, when she was just a sweet old lady with a walker.

When I told my friend Gregorij von Leitis, an accomplished theater director who has worked in theater all over the world for seven decades, that I cried before every speech about Maria, he said, "Don't do that. It's not effective." At first, I was defensive, saying it was unavoidable and that it makes the audience feel my genuineness.

"Trust me. Keep it together, and it will all come across," he affirmed.

I put that into practice, and it worked—at least when I could pull it off. Sometimes drippy cheeks were unavoidable.

The brunch talk was the big one hosted on Sydney Harbor at what I was told was a $50 million home. Lorna mentioned that some WIZO members didn't show up because they had been underwhelmed by past guest speakers. But after they heard about the success of this one they were "kicking themselves" for not attending. Lorna said my talk(s) had changed the game for WIZO NSW. With Molly Bloom booked as the keynote speaker in fall 2018, WIZO Sydney was looking at a burgeoning future for guest speakers. She messaged me through WhatsApp that night: "You made 120 Jewish ladies very happy today. That is no small feat."

Not only was I eternally connected to Di after our Facebook serendipity, her friend Sophie and I became fast spirit animals, and coupled with Lorna's magnetism and WIZO office manager Hagit's soulfulness, I had made four female friends in my life.

Every moment of Sydney was worth documenting, but there was one event I knew there was no way Maria could keep a straight face witnessing.

CHAPTER 19

The Synagogue

Part One

One day in 2010, as Maria and I sat breakfasting in her folksy Cheviot Hills bungalow, I told her that I was a quarter Jewish—my grandmother on my dad's side was Jewish, which I wasn't told until I was in my thirties. After she finished howling with laughter, she exclaimed, "Darling, you're about as Gentile as they come!" At that time, she was steadily losing her short-term memory, but that you're-about-as-Gentile-as-they-come story she always remembered with remarkable regularity.

So here was the deal. Lorna informed me weeks earlier that I would be speaking at a synagogue in Sydney. My attitude was "just tell me where to be, and I'll be there." But when on the night of, I found myself en route to the talk in an Uber with Di's kids Dean and Natalie telling me we were headed for the Central Synagogue—which I googled was *the largest synagogue in the southern hemisphere*—I was holy-shit nervous.

Minutes away from Central Synagogue, Dean turned around in the front seat and said: "You have your yarmulke, right?" *As if hearing about the giant synagogue wasn't enough to have a heart attack.* No, I didn't have my yarmulke, maybe because I wasn't Jewish. Dean grinned as he pulled a thick satin one out of his suit pocket and gave it to me. It was the first time I'd ever put one on.

I needed some quiet time before we arrived at the synagogue to figure out how I was going to make clear to a roomful of devotees who probably assumed I had spoken at dozens of synagogues that I was a professional synagogue speaker. Why else would I be at a synagogue if I had never spoken at one, let alone the *biggest synagogue in the southern freaking hemisphere*? The next question I had for myself was whether I needed to alter my content. In all my non-synagogue talks, the majority of guests were Jewish, but this was in an iconic place of worship, and I wasn't exactly a man of the cloth. What in God's name was I going to say to these people?

Well, at least I can fall back on my PowerPoint presentation. The thought sounded comforting. That is, until Diane, seeing me show up carrying my laptop, widened her eyes as if I were carrying a gun. "Don't let anyone see you with that," she said as she looked around nervously. She told me that because it was Shabbat (which traditionally lasts from Friday evening to Saturday night), it meant no technology of any kind was allowed anywhere near the synagogue, which meant the laptop I was carrying was suddenly contraband.

I was supposed to just *know* this? It's not as if Maria taught me how to be Jewish. Di even told me that you couldn't have a phone, a watch, and, it went without saying, a PowerPoint presentation. Oh, and you couldn't even have a pen on you. A *pen* was *technology*. What a clueless Gentile I was proving to be. I stashed my laptop in Di's car. I was officially stripped of everything except my yarmulke and my mouth.

The plan was that they would do the Shul service downstairs in the main room, and after that, the rabbi would announce there would be a special Shabbat dinner upstairs where anyone was welcome to come and hear the *special* guest speak.

Meantime, at least I had my inside man, fourteen-year-old Dean, who looked twenty-one and, at six two, was as tall as I am. He seemed to know what he was doing. As we filed into the pews, I stayed keen with Dean. I looked up at the balcony and noticed Di, Natalie, and all the rest of the women sitting together. On the lower level, where I was, sat all the men. *So that's why Di and Natalie mysteriously disappeared.*

Aside from Di, Dean, Natalie, and the rabbi, no one knew who I was. I was just a new guy with yellow pants and a blue button-down shirt, trying to fit in with a crowd mostly dressed in black and white. There was no reason I needed to be anyone but Gentile me, but I convinced myself I needed to act as if I were Jewish. I wasn't going to take the time to explain to a curious onlooker who I was and why I was wearing yellow pants, so pretending not to be me felt like the best way to go. I had my satin yarmulke on, I was rolling with keen Dean, and my phone was off and buried in my pocket. I was ready for my technology-free worship.

As the cantor began to sing, I casually looked around to see what everyone was doing. *Singing.* Duh. I wasn't going to sing, but I needed to find a prayer book. Dean, who was standing next to me, was crooning away. I grabbed a songbook out of the back of the pew in front of me. I squinted to see what page number Dean was on, but the print was so small and my leaning in felt so ridiculous that I ditched the notion of ever knowing the exact page number and threw open my book purposefully to a page I was determined to treat as the correct one.

I glanced up at Di and Natalie and pursed my lips like vintage Bill Clinton, as if I were successfully concealing my ineptitude. Diane made it clear that I wasn't, by leaning into her daughter's ear and whispering something that made them break into laughter. *Look at Gregor trying to be Jewish.* It put me in a more relaxed mood imagining Maria right there with them joining in the fun.

The entire time, I felt eyeballs to my left. I finally shot the man a John McCain smile and went back to my pretend singing. His eyeballs weren't diverting. I looked at him again to show him I wasn't ignoring him. "You know you're on the wrong page," he whispered. *As if that wasn't obvious?*

After the service finished, the rabbi made his announcements and mentioned the Shabbat dinner upstairs. When he pointed me out in the crowd, the nosey guy next to me in the pews patted me on the back and said he looked forward to my speech.

Out of about two hundred people at the service downstairs, roughly half showed up at the Shabbat dinner. First, we ate. But I didn't. I couldn't think about food, let alone eat it. I was too nervous. And by nervous I mean I was preparing myself for a public hanging.

When the dinner was nearing its end, about five minutes before I was to go up and speak, I had a realization that made me consider sneaking off and flying back to America.

CHAPTER 20

The Chuck Chapters

Part Three

There were times that Chuck at seventy-one had more trouble getting around than his ninety-four-year-old mother. It was a combination of his back, his eating what he wanted when he wanted it, and not exercising. Maria had a penchant for unhealthy eating—if it were up to her, she would have eaten Weisswurst and hazelnut ice cream for breakfast, lunch, and dinner—but the difference between her and her son was that she didn't turn into a twirling tornado if she didn't get what she wanted. Chuck did. If you got between him and his ice cream, you were in a battle you wouldn't win.

Chuck was clearly his mother's son when it came to exercise. Just two years earlier, when Tina the physical therapist would visit the house and put Maria through her exercise regimen, all Maria would want to do was socialize, like two bantering friends at a hair salon. "How is your new boyfriend?" Maria would ask her in the comfort of her chair, inciting any kind of distraction that would keep her from having to lift a finger.

Chuck, who inherited Tina from his mother, also inherited Maria's stall tactics. If he turned up his charm—and, trust me, at Chuck's best I'd never seen anyone more charming—he figured he would make it through the entire hour without Tina realizing they hadn't done anything. But it never happened that way. Tina was too sharp and too cute.

When I was caring for Chuck in 2014, one of the things I dreaded most was taking him on daily walks, because he didn't want anything to do with anything that was good for him. It took a herculean patience to get him out of the house, unless it was to go to the Cheesecake Factory in Beverly Hills—which I'll get to in a moment. Chuck's resistance to exercise was a depressing reminder of Maria toward the end. In the beginning, *she* would ask *me* to take a walk. But toward the end she would do anything not to have to get out of her chair or her bed. Chuck, at seventy-one, was following the same sad script. One time on a walk I had to leave him sitting on a ledge a half block away, walk back to the house, get in the car, drive the half block to pick him up, help him into the passenger seat, and coast home. That was a sad day.

It never helped that Chuck was the categorical opposite of a multitasker. He was a one-task-at-a-time type of guy—a lion stalking its prey. If he was involved in a task, it enveloped him to the degree that if you interrupted him, you interrupted a lion concentrating on its prey. For example, he loved comedian Mort Sahl and Credence Clearwater Revival front man John Fogerty. I never knew him to listen to any other artists. If you couldn't find him, he was probably in his office enjoying a vinyl record of Sahl doing a set or on his IBM computer watching a YouTube clip of Fogerty in concert. He was so intensely engrossed in these two acts that you couldn't just enter the room and start a conversation—at least not if you didn't want to see him leap out of his skin. You had to call him first on the phone. Then just hang up when he answered. After that, since his focus was broken by the ring, walking in was tension-free. And besides, a random hang-up to Chuck was as forgettable as an itch.

Chuck's intense focus oddly applied to fruit too. Before eating a banana, for example, he needed to focus every ounce of his energy on peeling each sticky strand off, as if he and those banana strands were the only two things on Earth. And when he went down to the garage to cut his toenails, if you happened to walk in on his unshakable focus clipping each nail to perfection, there was the concentrating lion. All this, in my eyes, spoke to his earnestness.

This is what it came down to with Chuck: you either loved him, feared him, or complained about him. Not many loved him. Most feared him. Everybody complained about him. I loved him and I complained about him, but I never feared him because I understood him. It needs to be said that I never saw Chuck lose his temper around his children Ken and Phil. His kids, from his perspective (and everyone else's), were saints to the point that Chuck, forever self-flagellating, always felt undeserving of them. He was proud to say that he owed anything good in his kids to their mother, Sheila.

There were things you learned quickly with Chuck. For example, his particularity with books. If you wanted to read anything from his personal collection, he expected you to leave his spines in flawless shape. But to preserve the spines to the perfection he demanded, one would have to crack a book barely open, like you were peeking through an ajar door at a sleeping baby. And with most of his books having small typeface—mainly small, paperback thrillers—peeking through an ajar door wouldn't cut it. You couldn't read what you couldn't see. So no one ever touched his books, a win for everyone. Of course, the only reason I knew all this was because when I first moved in I got a tongue-lashing for opening one of his books at a normal width.

Another thing you learned quickly was not to put things on chairs. If you wanted a guaranteed scolding from Chuck, you would set your coat or bag of groceries on a chair.

"Chairs are for sitting!" he would yell if he saw anything but a butt on a chair. No one was immune to Chuck's chair rule, not even Maria.

His newspaper was another thing he was unreasonable about. In the morning, if he found his perfectly smooth and untouched *Los Angeles Times* the slightest bit crumpled, you would wake up *real* quick. Or if he found out you ate directly out of the ice cream carton—he had an eagle eye for the telltale spoon marks—you would wish you were dead. He caught me doing the latter once, and if you offered me $10,000 dollars to do it again, I would have said, "Are you nuts?"

And, by the way, if you put that spoon you used to decimate his ice cream carton into the dishwasher spoon-side down instead of spoon-side up, like most people do, it would not have been pretty. To this day, I put in every piece of silverware, save sharp knives, eating-side up, all because Chuck said it cleaned them much better. (It's actually a very brilliant thing that every clean-seeking human should get in the habit of doing.)

And then there were the waiters. God help you if you had to wait on Chuck—for example, when he ordered his iced tea. Chuck was famous for this at his home-away-from-home, the Cheesecake Factory in Beverly Hills. He ate there almost every day, ordering the same thing: chicken Caesar salad, followed by a plate of tiramisu, thereby cancelling out any chance at a healthy meal.

"I would like ice filled to the very top of the glass," Chuck would calmly begin his instruction to the waiter. "Now when I say top, I mean top. Okay?"

The waiter would nod as if he'd done this a thousand times. And Donna and I would sit there thinking, "Oh, if he only knew what was coming."

"Now," Chuck would resume, "you're going to think that's all you have to do. But after you fill that packed glass of ice with the iced tea, that ice will naturally go down a bit. You understand?" He would wait until the waiter understood the physics of it. "That leaves more space for more ice, yes? So after the tea is in there with the ice, I want you to fill it up *again* with ice, so it's really packed tight in there, almost heaping over the top. It may take you a few times."

It rarely happened that a waiter who was assigned to Chuck wasn't one who knew him well. The managers knew never to stick him with a newbie. But newbie or not, Chuck would never degrade a waiter for any reason. Chuck yelled at his brothers and his mother, maybe a really nasty person he met—definitely me, for slamming his car door too forcefully—but he drew the line with waiters for some reason. Chuck had a kind of altruism for the service industry. This is probably due to his mother, who always treated every service person she encountered like a friend. And Chuck put his money where his mouth was. He tipped well: thirty percent. Sometimes forty. He gave twenty-dollar Christmas gifts to every waiter and bus boy at the restaurant every year.

You have to understand something: Chuck wasn't on edge. As enraged as he could get over the littlest of things, he wasn't looking to ruffle anybody's feathers. He didn't go around with a chip on his shoulder, he didn't think he was dealt a bad hand or that anyone was out to get him. He was the most grateful person on Earth, constantly in awe of how lucky he was to have such a great mother who afforded him such a great life. You could even call him a humanitarian. But he was an accidental hornet's nest. If he got bumped … there was that monster within he couldn't control.

Which is why everyone walked on eggshells around him. But what made him such a complex character study was that he was doing the same thing around you. He was so acutely aware of how much he rubbed people the wrong way without realizing it, that he always figured someone was in a sour mood because of something he did or said. Chuck apologized more than Larry David does on *Curb Your Enthusiasm*. He may not have cared what people thought of him, but he wanted to please everybody. Most of the time he fell short.

Around age forty, Chuck was in a session with his psychiatrist. When he left that office an hour later, his life would never be the same again.

CHAPTER 21

The Synagogue

Part Two

Back at the synagogue, I had a major problem on my hands.

In order to read the Shabbat-goers a poem I had written Maria for her ninety-fourth birthday—a part of the talk I couldn't bring myself to omit—I needed to access my phone to be able to read it to them, since I didn't have it memorized or written down anywhere. But because, hello-hello, I couldn't use any technology, *including a pen!* I was in a real bind. I started to panic. Any minute I was going to have to get up there and speak!

I turned to the person next to me—who shall remain nameless to protect their identity—and explained I absolutely had to have a pen or I couldn't do the talk. The person scanned the room to make sure no one was looking, dug into a purse (okay, it was a female), slipped me a pen, and whispered tensely, "Go out of the room and do it. Hurry. You're on in five minutes." I snuck the pen into my pocket and headed for the door like Chuck on a good day: calm, cool, collected.

When I closed the door behind me, I went from Chuck Altmann to Usain Bolt. The place was huge, and I had a million hallways to choose from. *Which one is empty?* I sprinted down the main marble stairs, across the foyer, snagged a pamphlet thingy I saw on a table, booked it down a side hallway, found a quiet corner, dropped onto the red velvet carpet, propped my back against the wall, yanked out my phone and the infamous pen, and started madly scribbling on the pamphlet so fast I could barely read my own handwriting.

At times, I heard clicking footsteps on the marble foyer floors and would freeze as if I were in danger of being arrested by the Shabbat police—they were on to me. When the sounds dissipated, I'd resume my scribbling. It took nearly ten minutes to finish writing the poem. I sprinted back to the Shabbat dinner, expecting to find everyone wondering where the hell I was.

Reentering the room slightly out of breath, I made immediate eye contact with the woman who lent me the pen. I nodded to her: "Mission accomplished." She nodded back: "I knew you could do it." The rabbi was passing around scotch to all the tables. When he saw I had returned, he headed for the front of the room. My stomach dropped to my feet.

Thirty seconds later, the beguiling Rabbi Wolf and I stood arm in arm at the front of the room as he introduced me: "Did you ever think you'd be speaking at a shul, Gregor?" The attendees breaking out into laughter was my answer. As I looked out on all the curious faces wondering what this yellow-panted Gentile had to say about the Jewish woman who got that famous painting back, I knew I was in the right synagogue.

Below is that poem. What made it so meaningful back in 2010 after I read it to Maria on her ninety-forth birthday at her son Jim's house, she said with tears in her eyes, "Darling, my kids don't even know about some of these details." It was the first and only time I ever saw Maria Altmann cry.

> A charmed and fairly-tale life she's had;
> From Klimt to Adele to her wonderful dad;
> From butlers to opera to her dear Uncle Ferry;
> To the smart handsome man she'd eventually marry;
> From Satin to rabbits to the horses she'd pity;
> Who'd slip on the ice that surrounded the city;
> From wedding and parties and galas galore;
> To the roaster of chestnuts she'd love to adore;

There's no end in sight to the people she's known;
To the places she's been and the courage she's shown;
And yes one more thing I have failed to yet mention;
A case so supreme that it gave quite a pension;
But strip away all the above that I've told;
The fame and the fortune … the Lady in Gold;
And that which remains is a powerful light;
The most wonderful, whimsical, grand dame in sight.
And I know I'm right!

I have secured the title of my next book: *The Geriatric Journeys of a Gentile Judaist.*

Release year: 2028. (The woman who gave me the pen was the great Diane Symonds)

CHAPTER 22

The Chuck Chapters

Part Four

IBM originally hired Chuck as a salesman. During a boardroom meeting with his first major client, after the client explained what they wanted, they directed a question at Chuck: "So can you do that for us?"

Chuck's response: "There's no way in hell I can do that for you."

Naturally, IBM lost the client. It was now no longer a secret at the company that Chuck wasn't a salesman. First of all, he didn't understand the "well here's what we *can* do for you." That kind of sales talk wasn't in Chuck's vocabulary. He couldn't think on his feet, he wasn't flexible, and he had no filter. He had everything it took to be a salesman on paper—he was handsome, he had a magnetic smile that lit up a room, and he spoke with a resonant, inflective, James Coburn-esque voice perfect for slinging entertaining yarns. But all that was out the window the moment he just couldn't hold back the truth. (I remember Maria always telling me with a straight face: "Chuck has never told a lie.")

Instead of firing him, IBM stuck him in a corner office behind a computer. He would work as a successful engineer for the next thirty years.

The person who told me this story was Chuck.

One of my favorite pastimes with Maria became one of my favorites with our former IBM salesman—floating into his room first thing in the morning, sitting down at the foot of his bed, and milking that indescribably intimate time of day when the first person one sees is the person they didn't share a bed with. Here is where enchanting stories of days bygone were shared. Chuck always had one for me about his mother that I hadn't heard or one that I'd heard but was told in a different way.

Back when I had finished the manuscript to part one, the first readers were Maria's kids. Margie, Jim, and Peter finished it within a couple weeks, and all ardently approved. I had purposely put off giving the book to Chuck, for the same reason one might put off visiting a dentist, or a CPA. But I needed to get my cavity filled, and my taxes were long overdue. And without Chuck's approval, there was no book. There would never be a book. I gave it to him one evening. My phone rang early the next morning.

"Hello?" I answered.

"Thanks to you, I was up all night reading your book."

Holy shit. He read the whole thing in one night.

And then, silence.

Most people fill awkward silences with small talk, maybe a sigh, but Chuck rode out dead silences for as long as he wanted, unapologetically. All I knew was the last three years of work, my future as a memoirist, hung in the balance with his next words.

"You did my mother justice."

He went on and on about how I managed to capture his mother's essence. He even told me, "Gregor, you made the last three years of my mother's life worth living." That was one of the most affecting things anyone has ever told me.

You see, you didn't go to Chuck for hope. If you wanted hope, you went to Maria. You went to Chuck for the truth. Chuck's review of my book is still, to this day, the one I'm most proud of. Screw the *New York Times,* you need Charles Gustav Altmann's endorsement if you want to be taken seriously in this world.

One day in the early eighties, around age forty, Chuck was in a session with his psychiatrist. At the end of the hour, he handed Chuck an essay titled *Understanding Asperger's Syndrome*—his way of telling Chuck that he had Asperger's. This essay affected Chuck deeply. "Every single thing in that article described me to a T," he said to me.

This wasn't a bad thing. It was kind of a good thing. Chuck finally had a way out of his pain: science. And he had an alibi: biology. It wasn't his fault. It was beyond his control. He must have walked out of that office feeling a sense of purpose for the first time in his life.

After reading that article, it all made sense to him. He had never been able to read social cues and expressions. He took everything you said literally. He hated social gatherings because he couldn't fully understand subtleties in character, nuances in intention, and therefore could never be sensitive to it. He was brutally honest to a fault (e.g., his stint as an IBM salesman), and read people's emotions in black and white. To Chuck, someone was either in a happy mood or a sad mood. Every last scratch on his car needed buffing; every last stain on his shirt needed removing. His hobbies: aviation and coding. Even times where you ended a sentence with the obligatory, "You know what I mean?" and it was perfectly clear to everyone what you meant, he would *never* go along with it until you explained exactly what you meant with zero nuance. He wasn't being difficult, he wasn't being ignorant … he was just being Chuck.

But I saw Chuck as a blessing, just as his small group of friends saw him—people like Kirk, an old IBM colleague, and Bruce, someone he'd met on Craigslist to fix his computer. We all got him. We all loved him exactly how he came. We wanted to strangle him a lot, but at the end of the day he would always have a get-out-of-jail-free card with us.

Greta Thunberg, a sixteen-year-old Swedish climate change activist with Asperger's who was in the news in September 2019 for standing up to this mocking tweet by Trump—"She seems like a very happy young girl looking forward to a bright and beautiful future. So nice to see!"—wrote this in retaliation of the tweet and other degrading comments hurled at her: "Some people mock me for my diagnosis. But Asperger is not a disease, it's a gift." And she went on to describe that gift. I saw Chuck like I see Greta: as a gift.

Not everything on Fairburn Avenue was so serious. We had our fun. Once, Donna went out of town for a few days on a cruise with Bruce. Chuck and I were sitting in the cat's lair, a room Donna had reserved for her Siamese cats, Havoc and Butler. Just outside on the back balcony lived her two parakeets, one a youngster and the other an oldster. Tina had just left after a workout with Chuck. As we sat in the lair chatting, we both heard a rustle and then a thump.

The odd sound intrigued Chuck enough to get him out of his chair to investigate. I followed him out to the back balcony, and we peered into the parakeet cage. The youngster was happily perched on his swing post, while the oldster lay motionless on the cage floor.

Chuck couldn't let it go. What weighed on him wasn't the fact that the bird had died; it was the fear that Donna would somehow find a way to pin it on him. Maybe Chuck had made a sudden movement or yelled so loudly that the bird fell to its death. He knew how much Donna loved her animals, and he also knew how much anything he did for her never seemed to be done quite right.

So he needed to do the right thing with this bird, and neither of us knew what that was. We decided the bird would go into a paper bag and into the freezer. Maybe Donna would come home from her trip and, seeing the frozen bird was in good enough condition to have a proper burial, would exonerate us of any crime.

When Donna returned home, the first thing Chuck did before even saying hello was to tell her, "Something happened while you were gone." He was calm on the outside, but on the inside I could tell he was a rubber band ball ready to snap. "Gregor, go get our friend out of the freezer," he instructed.

Donna watched curiously as I reentered the room with a paper bag and handed it to her. She opened it up and widened her eyes as she pulled the frozen bird out. While she studied it with astonishment, he told her every last detail of the story, down to the time of day we found him dead. She completely surprised us by saying she expected him to be dead long ago. He was twenty-three, which is 103 in human years. She actually found our freezer decision kind of amusing. I was relieved and Chuck was elated. He could live another day.

But he was nearing his end of days, and there were no U-turn signs in sight.

About a month or two after the bird incident, the day he died, I was downstairs in my room. It was early evening, after we had eaten dinner in the dining room. As I later found out from Donna, she and Chuck were upstairs in bed watching *The Bachelor* on television, when an argument ensued. Donna wanted to stick with the *The Bachelor* and Chuck wanted to watch anything *but The Bachelor.*

Suddenly, Donna ran to the top of the stairs, screaming: "Gregor, help, help! Come up here!"

I sprinted upstairs into their room and found Chuck doubled over in his bed in a near-unconscious state. His body was swaying back and forth and he was mumbling, his eyes barely open. "We were arguing about what to watch," she yelled in a panic, "and then he just … He just keeled over!"

We both tried to shake him out of his catatonia, but nothing seemed to work. He was moaning, his face was turning purple, and his eyes were starting to glaze over. Donna grabbed the phone and called the paramedics. They arrived a few minutes later and slid him off the bed onto the floor to perform CPR. No pulse. He was pronounced dead almost immediately. *Massive heart attack.*

I sat in the hallway calling every Altmann I had in my phone.

CHAPTER 23

Road Trip!

Part One

It was July 2014, and Chuck, a month shy of his seventy-fourth birthday, just couldn't stand being away from his mother any longer. As he reunited with his new roommate in the sky, I was stuck on the ground with mine, a scenario neither Donna nor I pretended was ideal. Together in a five-thousand-square-foot, five-bedroom, five-bathroom house that looked like a monopoly game version of the Getty Museum, no amount of square footage, not even the real-life 150,000-square-foot Getty Museum in Brentwood could have been enough space to justify Chuck's wife and I living under the same roof.

The reality was, Donna and I were both stubborn, passionate, and tough to live with. Chuck was too, but I loved Chuck. I couldn't make myself love Donna. She did a lot of good for a lot of people. She took good care of her 96-year-old mother, she spent her days volunteering as a docent at the Petersen Automotive Museum, and she was always buying gifts for Chuck's grandchildren. She was in service to a lot of people. She really did love Chuck, in her own way, but Chuck loved her far more than she could ever love him. He loved Donna-Marie Altmann more than any other woman aside from his mother, and that was a fact. And that's what helped us all feel better, knowing that he was at his happiest when he was with her.

At any rate, I had to move out of the miniature Getty ASAP. But where would I go? Wherever that was, I was free. I had no obligations and nowhere to be. Aside from a six-week gig that Summer producing a reality TV show down in Myrtle Beach called *Welcome to Myrtle Manor,* my only job had been to care for Chuck.

Out of all the things I packed into my Toyota Scion, maybe the most important thing was a stack of pages that said: "The Accidental Caregiver: Stage Play."

Along with a crazy thought.

Weeks prior on Twitter I'd exchanged a few tweets with a British theater director and dramaturge based in London named Alice Kornitzer. I mentioned my book and that I was working on turning it into a stage play. I told her I had never written a play and that when I was done I would value her feedback. In the meantime, I sent her the book.

Wednesday, July 13, 2014 came, and I had typed "End of play" on the last page of the script. I reached back out to Alice. In the interim, she had read my book and had good things to say. I sent her the play and was surprised to hear back just two days later. She thought it had serious potential as a theater piece and she wanted to direct it. Things were getting serious, so we moved to Skype. She was twenty-six years old; had a thick head of black, flowing hair; spoke fluent German; and was kind, charming, and brilliant—Maria would have adored her. And as you know, Maria didn't adore women.

In my correspondences with Alice, I had alluded to my transitional living situation and how I'd been feeling a persistent nudging to move to the Big Apple to bring Maria to life on stage. The idea excited her. She had never directed a play outside of Europe, let alone in the greatest theater city in the world, and had been pining for the perfect project. I told her I had very little money to spend on the play itself and that I couldn't pay her.

She decided that if we secured a venue and a theater run, she would fly to New York on her own dime and direct the play. I would only need to cover her expenses. And it turns out she had a friend she could stay with in Brooklyn, so I didn't need to worry about her rent. We had no cast, no venue, and no clue how we were going to do it, but we knew that whatever outcome our meeting would bring would be a defining moment in our lives. I told her I'd reach out to some theater venues and get back to her on the road.

On Sunday, July 17, I sent a flurry of emails to theaters and festivals in New York. Then I packed everything I owned—which was basically just clothing, bedding and artwork—and stuffed it into my white Toyota Scion XA. I brought up the 90 East on my phone's map. I had nowhere specific to stay in New York, but that was the least of my worries. In fact, I had no worries. I had the open road and no pressure to speed down it.

(Speaking of speeding, I ended up getting two tickets in South Dakota. Both times I got off. On one of the times, the cop let me go after finding out I was an actor from California. Sometimes it pays to be an actor.)

CHAPTER 24

Road Trip!

Part Two

One of the first calls I made on the road was to Maria's son Peter, who lived in Tacoma with his wife, *Sea*Donna. I told him about my spontaneous move to New York spawned by both my desire to break free of *LA*Donna and my drive to let even more people know his mother existed. From my standpoint I wanted to introduce Maria to every single person in the world, but I was also sensitive to the fact that no Altmann had ever asked me to do any of this. I wasn't letting the latter weigh me down, though. This was my mission and my life. Peter and all the kids understood how much their mother loved me and I loved her, and therefore stood by whatever I did. And if I dealt my cards right, my play would debut before the release of *Woman in Gold,* which I recently read had gone into production in England. Peter and I agreed it was a perfect time for me to drive up the Pacific Coast Highway and visit them before I took a hard right and embarked on my cross-country adventure.

Fifteen years earlier, after I graduated from Florida State University, I hopped into my Green Geo Storm and took the 40 West (the bottom portion of the country) to Los Angeles to start my new life as a reality television producer. And now, in 2014, I would drive the top portion and head East, beginning at Peter's Puget Sound, a magical place I remember Maria always saying reminded her of the lakes and trees of her youth in Austria.

Incredibly, after living in LA for fifteen years, I had never driven beyond Malibu on the PCH. I charted my drive: Santa Barbara, Big Sur,

San Francisco, the redwoods, the Oregon beaches, Portland, Seattle, then Tacoma—all destinations I had never before checked off my bucket list.

When I arrived in Tacoma four days later, I greeted one of the world's foremost bear-huggers, Peter Altmann. In 2010, when I had flown up to Tacoma with Maria for her last big trip outside of California, Peter and Donna were living in a house a few miles from Puget. Now they had one literally on it.

Peter's boat, *The Pacific Mutsea*—an ode to Maria's nickname, Mutzi—was still in full working order. Boarding it reminded me of that memorable afternoon four years earlier when we boated to the house of Jim Valley (a member of the 1960s' rock band Paul Revere and the Raiders, and a good friend of Peter's) and set up a walking plank at shore to transport Maria off the boat on a rickety wooden chair without getting her feet wet.

Peter, Donna, and I boated around Peaceful Puget, snowcapped Mount Rainier looming in the background. Occasionally we'd spot a whiskered seal bobbing its jolly head curiously above the still water's surface. It was so peaceful that there was a kind of uneasy ease to it, the feeling that I was safe and loved but that I was about to embark on something so important, I wasn't sure I could handle it. Donna and Peter spoiled me like a son. Donna had a teenage son, and Peter never had any kids, which always confounded me that such a sweet man who would make such a great father didn't have a child who could look up to him. But I looked up to him. Donna was the sweetest woman in Washington, and it was only fitting she married one of the sweetest men I knew. The end came too soon. I wanted to stay Puget-bound forever. As I pulled away from paradise, I looked through my rearview mirror to see Peter and Donna huddling together lovingly watching me drive away. My life right now was one big Hallmark movie.

As I found the correct highway headed east, I thought to myself: "Who do I know in New York?" Soon Victoria, the daughter of Maria's cousin Ruth Rogers-Altmann, flashed in my mind. You might recall from part one that Ruth is Maria's cousin by marriage—she was the wife of Hans Altmann, the son of Fritz's brother Bernhard Altmann, of Altmann Cashmere Sweaters. In 2010, while in Los Angeles caring for Maria, after I told her I wanted to see her aunt Adele's gold portrait in New York at the Neue Galerie, she picked up the phone and called her ninety-three-year-old cousin Ruth and asked her if her friend Gregor could stay with her for the weekend. Of course he could. It was on that weekend that I met her daughter Victoria.

I decided to call Victoria, but before I did, since four years had elapsed, I prepared myself to hear that Ruth had died. I was relieved to find out that she hadn't, and in fact was doing very well. Since her husband Hans died fifteen years earlier, Ruth, ninety-six now, had been living alone in her rent-controlled two-bedroom apartment on Park Avenue and Thirty-Ninth Street, in a Midtown Manhattan neighborhood called Murray Hill. Victoria expressed concern about her mother not having anyone living with her, as she was starting to do things like leave the stove on or misplace her house keys, and she could no longer leave her apartment without supervision. Ruth's granddaughter Alexandra, who lived in Brooklyn, visited as often as she could, but it wasn't the same as having someone living there.

My potentially living with Ruth had not clicked in either of our heads yet, so I told Victoria I wasn't sure where I would be living. That's when the light bulb suddenly went off for us. If I was up for it, Victoria eventually ardently offered, I could live with her mother rent-free in exchange for being a man-around-the-house. I reassured her I was a good stove-turner-offer and an even better walker. Boom. I had a place to stay in New York. *Things fall into place when you follow your heart.*

Knowing I'd have a lot of other things on my plate, i.e., unveiling Maria to audiences on stage, Victoria made it clear that I wasn't Ruth's caregiver. I was merely her roommate, who when home or when I had time, could food shop with her, make her meals, and take her for walks. *Maria, Chuck, and now Ruth.* I was in a flow I couldn't begin to explain.

Somewhere driving through Montana I heard back from a theater festival in New York called the Venus Adonis Theater Festival. My script had been chosen for entry. YES! I would be responsible for bringing them a fully cast, ready-to-perform play, and they would in turn provide the marketing and the venue—the respected Off Broadway Robert Moss Theater, across from the famed Public Theater in East Village. I drafted an email to Alice and pressed as much passion as I could into the send button. She replied a day later with her plane ticket confirmation. She was set to arrive in New York on December 15.

It was happening.

After a few hours on the road, I found myself in a seductive trance coasting through the flat basins and treeless plateaus of the great Continental Divide, a far cry from the future concrete jungles of New York. Yellowstone National Park, spanning 3,500 square miles and two million acres, was in my sights.

I ended my park exploration with Old Faithful, checking out a few spurts before I headed for the exit. But little did I know, unforeseen danger lay in waiting.

CHAPTER 25

You Still Talk About Me, Darling?

GREGOR. Why am I still talking about you?

MARIA. You still talk about me? But I'm so boring.

GREGOR. You saw me in Australia. I speak at retirement communities, private homes, synagogues.

MARIA. Synagogues? You're going to make me laugh.

GREGOR. You're already laughing.

MARIA. You're about as—

GREGOR. Gentile as they come!

MARIA. What do you say about me?

GREGOR. You know what I say. You read the first book, right? About our time together? I showed you a few passages before I published it.

MARIA. Yes, but what do you say about me in your talks? I wasn't around for those.

GREGOR. How one morning in the kitchen you saw an old apple and you picked it up and you examined it and said, "This is so old it's a schoolmate of mine."

MARIA. That sounds like something I'd say. What else?

GREGOR. That time you asked me: "Isn't there some species of animal where the male has sex with the female and then kills her?" And I was like,

"I don't know," and you were like, "Well it's a good idea."

MARIA. You tell it so funny.

GREGOR. Or when you said, "I don't believe in ghosts … but that doesn't mean I want one in my room."

MARIA. I didn't say that.

GREGOR. The point is I'm still going around telling people how incredible you are. I don't understand why. Why can't I just move on?

MARIA. Well, it's not about me.

GREGOR. Of course it's about you. Without you, I wouldn't be doing it.

MARIA. Maybe it was about me in the beginning, but not now. Let's eat, darling. I'm hungry. Do we have any hazelnut ice cream?

GREGOR. Why haven't I been able to find a love that touches me as deeply as yours?

MARIA. Because I'm up here making sure it doesn't happen. I'm only having fun with you, sweetheart. This desire of yours—to go around and speak about us. It's not to show people who I am. That's boring. It's to show who you are. The fire inside you to connect, to love, to inspire.

GREGOR. I miss seeing you write things.

MARIA. Write things? What do you mean?

GREGOR. Remember that note Plácido Domingo gave you after you met him backstage at Das Rheingold? He signed his name really flamboyantly, and you said, "He must think *nothing* of himself." And then you came down with that cold the next day. We were so glad it happened the next day. How is heaven by the way? Are they treating you well?

MARIA. But darling, do you still have the note?

GREGOR. I think Margie has it.

MARIA. I miss Margie. We had so many fun phone conversations. Is she still in Hawaii?

GREGOR. Yes. She didn't want to tell you she moved because she didn't want you to worry.

MARIA. Are you still acting?

GREGOR. It's your defense mechanism.

MARIA. What is?

GREGOR. Changing the subject when things get serious. You're addicted to titillating conversations, and when it has a hint of getting boring or dark, you change the subject.

MARIA. Gregor, I want you to go have fun and find someone you love. I give you permission. You're going to make someone very happy.

CHAPTER 26

Road Trip!

Part Three

As I was crawling along in traffic to exit Yellowstone, I found myself an increasingly large distance from the car in front of me. I checked my rearview. The car behind me was practically kissing my bumper. How did this happen, that I hadn't paid enough attention to notice how far I'd lagged behind? That no one honked at me was a miracle. I expected everyone to be as impatient as I would have been.

Suddenly, a large, hairy shape flashed out of the corner of my eye, plodded out into the middle of the road, planted its hooves, and locked its eyes on me through the windshield.

I slammed on my breaks and sat frozen behind the wheel as I stared at a wild animal I was convinced would charge me at any moment. He was completely still, probably wondering the same thing about me. Somehow I relaxed enough to pull out my phone and snap a picture. I had seen wolves, deer, sheep, and even a moose on my trip through Yellowstone, but this was my first encounter with a big, bad bison, who wanted me to stay and have a shot of tequila with him.

He was an obstinate SOB, holding his ground as I inched towards him in my pathetic 4-Cylinder Toyota Scion. My inching wasn't doing anything to scare him. And there wasn't any room to pull around him, unless I wanted to drive into areas I wasn't sure weren't covering mushy swamps.

Not caring there was a line of cars going back at least a mile, the bison seemed to trade his stubbornness for playfulness by shuffling his feet and looking at me as if to say, "What else ya got?"

Suddenly, he seemed bored, turned, and started dawdling away. *Was he showing me the way out?* He remained in the middle of the road, so I tried to turn to pass him on the right, but before I could, he swerved into my path, forcing me to slam on my breaks. When I gunned it and swerved to his left, he did the same thing. This big, hairy beast wasn't going to let me leave. I checked my rearview and threw up my arms at the people behind me. They returned the gesture, as if they didn't know whether to laugh or call a forest ranger.

I had to get out of this national park. It was do or die. I revved the engine to startle him, floored it to the right and then quickly to the left and safely around him, faking him out. I WON. As I checked my rearview, I saw that the bison, having let me slip through the cracks, stood in front of the car behind me ready to play the game again with the next fool. Was he going to do this with every car trying to exit? It wasn't my concern now. I breathed a sigh of relief as I found the turnpike.

It was getting dark, and my driving thigh was killing me, but I pushed it until I got to Billings, Montana, where I pulled into a Cracker Barrel and had dinner. A cute waitress named Britney helped me. We added each other on Facebook and then never spoke again. Seemed about right. I tried to find a good hotel, but it was nearing midnight and they were all booked up. I parked my car in a parking lot and slept in a cramped yoga pose for about four hours. It was horribly uncomfortable, but the discomfort was usurped by a euphoric feeling that this whole trip was a choice, and I was determined to love every moment of it.

CHAPTER 27

Ruth

Part One

I'd visited New York several times over the years. I wasn't oblivious to the pandemonium set to unfold in my world. But what I experienced on September 28, 2014, as I wrapped up my cross-country road trip and turned off FDR Drive into the belly of my new home, was another story. I was in my car on Thirty-Ninth and First, headed three blocks away to Thirty-Ninth and Park. It took me *forty minutes* to navigate those three blocks. Later that evening, when I finally had time to get to a Starbucks to use the internet, I learned President Obama had been visiting the UN down the street, arriving virtually the same time I had, making an already overcrowded city something out of Armageddon. Which brought up another thing: Ruth didn't have Wi-Fi. Looks like Starbucks was going to be my office for the foreseeable future.

All because of the forty-fourth president, there wasn't one open parking spot in Midtown, so I double-parked and met Ruth's daughter Victoria standing with the burly doorman in front of 71 Park Avenue. I had met Victoria once, briefly, four years ago when I stayed with Ruth the weekend I visited New York to see the *Gold Portrait*. I remembered Victoria was a sculptor and an art historian and, as I discovered later via Wikipedia, had written a book in the 1990s about the sculptor Augustus Rodin, which solidified her as one of the world's foremost experts of his work—if a Rodin was not featured in her book, it wasn't an authentic Rodin.

Ruth was a painter and a fashion designer and the daughter of Austrian architect Arnold Karplus. Victoria's daughter Alexandra, who I'd also met four years ago, is an actress and a Pilates instructor, rounding out a family of artists. Victoria and I hugged quickly. We had work to do before I got my first parking ticket in New York. The doorman and I unloaded my packed-to-the-brim Scion, as Victoria kept an eagle eye on ticketers. Lucky for the doorman and me, there were no bulky items like furniture, only blankets, clothes and artwork, and, of course, my signed Klimt print, on which Maria wrote in November of 2010: "If we had met earlier, I would have been tempted to give you the original. Thank you for being so good to me. Love, Maria."

Ruth lived on the sixth floor of a prewar high-rise building located on the East side of Park Avenue between Thirty-Eighth and Thirty-Ninth Streets. It was a mere five-minute walk from Grand Central Station and a short seven-minute walk to Bryant Park. She had for the most part lived there since leaving Vienna in the 1930s, in a two-bedroom, two-bath condo she had chosen never to buy. She was on some serious rent control, paying around eight hundred dollars a month. For a condo like hers today, in a prime area of Manhattan like Murray Hill, I was told her apartment could easily rent for eight thousand dollars. Good ol' Ruth may have had the best deal in all of Manhattan.

After the doorman and I finished lugging my things through the green-marbled entryway and up the groaning elevator, Victoria and I stood in front of Ruth's heavy, hulking apartment door. *Knock-knock.* Moments later, we heard the sound of multiple locks banging back and forth, and finally the creaky door cracked open about as wide as you could open Chuck's books. When Ruth recognized her daughter, she opened it fully and wondered right away who the tall strange man standing next to her was. Victoria introduced me as the man who took care of her cousin Maria in California and had stayed with her that one weekend in 2010. Victoria mentioned, as if quickly slipping it in before

Ruth could put up a protest, that I would be living with her. To our surprise, Ruth had zero questions. She invited us in.

Ruth was essentially living in an art studio of her own art. She was prolific as a painter. Victoria told me she had painted around four hundred works. Every inch of wall space was covered with vibrant-colored paintings, mostly beach scenes painted at the Art Barge in East Hampton. Because she also worked in fashion, her closets were jammed with name clothing from around the world, outfits by designers like Yves Saint Laurent, Missoni, and Marimekko. She also had an entire closet full of Japanese kimonos. She collected African masks and sculptures, as well as porcelain and crystal table sets, and she owned four original ceramic Pablo Picasso plates and vases she had bought in the seventies from Picasso's actual studio in Cote d'Azur in the South of France. Did Ruth meet Picasso himself on any of her visits there? Ruth didn't recall, but Victoria said it was more likely she had met Jules Agard, his potter, who worked closely with Picasso.

Being in New York gave me a euphoric feeling that I was exactly where I was supposed to be. Of *course* I was meant to call Victoria, which led to our minds thinking the exact same thing, which led to seeing Ruth again and living with her and keeping her on Earth as long as possible. But I was faced with an immediate decision that had nothing to do with Ruth: where I would keep my car.

Everyone who knew anything about New York told me to sell it—if I wanted to travel somewhere, I could rent one. But I was stubborn. I was special, you see. I was going to be the only non-millionaire resident ever to figure out a way to park my car in Manhattan. After five days equaling nearly a hundred dollars in parking fees, I capitulated. I sold the car on Craigslist to a guy in Brooklyn. I forgot my golf clubs were in the back, and I never got a call, so it looks like he thought the clubs came with the car. I needed new ones anyway. Maybe I'd buy them with the money I'd save in parking. For the first time since I was sixteen, I was car-less.

Living with a 96-year-old woman took some getting used to. In the beginning, in order for Ruth to get acclimated to having me around the house, every morning I made sure to crack open her bedroom door and wave to her while she was lying in bed. I also wrote a note and taped it next to her old Pacific Bell wall phone: "Gregor is the man who lives with you. His telephone number is …"

There was an interesting dilemma that developed early on. Ruth had the habit of walking into my room without knocking. She had lived at 71 Park for fifty years. She'd gone in and out of that room tens of thousands of times. Suddenly, one day a strange man was living there. In my defense, though, it was a bit unnerving for me to be lying in bed or getting out of the shower and suddenly having Ruth open the door and awkwardly staring at me. Something needed to be done. Victoria suggested I write a note and tape it to my door, saying: "Please knock before entering." I did and signed it, "The man who lives here."

The first time I tested the plan I sat on my bed around the time she got up in the morning, bracing myself for another knock-less walk-in. I heard footsteps along the old creaking wooden floors gradually approach my room, and then they suddenly stopped. It was a pulse pounding few moments, as if there were a person with a gun who at any minute could burst through the door. I could feel and hear her reading the sign silently to herself. Soon the footsteps began creaking again, but this time farther and farther away. It worked! I was so proud of her! I called Victoria with the good news. After a while, Ruth didn't even need to walk up to the door to read the note. She knew not to go down that hallway. Finally, I took the note down, never to be an issue again.

We did our food shopping at the D'Agostino's on Third Avenue. Ruth had the habit of putting everything into plastic bags—not just fruit and vegetables but things like jars of jelly and boxes of cereal. I remembered her plastic bag fetish from when I visited New York years ago to see the gold portrait. I went along with her as if it was completely normal: "Oh, you want to put the jar of mustard in a bag?

Okay. Perfect." When we arrived at the checkout counter, we had a cart full of plastic bags. The lady smiled as if she was very familiar with Ruth and her plastic bag predilection.

It was October 2014, and guess who was arriving soon?

CHAPTER 28

Alice in Wonderland

Part One

Alice and I were scheduled to meet a block from Ruth's at a downstairs hole-in-the-wall pub called The Shakespeare, a meeting place that couldn't have been more appropriate for a theater professional from London. As I made my way down the stairs and into the dingy foyer, there stood *the* Alice Kornitzer, her angelic face and rosy cheeks just as cute and red as in her pictures.

We hugged like two people who had known each other for years. Maria had brought me yet another special human, and Alice and I almost immediately discovered that our personalities and biting senses of humor matched. She had a much more knowing smile than a woman of twenty-six years, and her polished way of speaking, what she described to me as BBC English, had me falling in creative love immediately. We got a table, ordered a pint, and got down to business.

I told her I had hired a casting director, Robin Carus, who was fairly well known in the Off Broadway world we'd be living in with the caregiver play. Robin was too expensive for me, but after I pitched her the story and sent her the script, she agreed to take a significant pay cut to be a part of it. And on top of that, she was Jewish, which only accentuated her interest in a story that centered around a Jewish woman. January 26, 2015, was our premiere date. We had a mere four weeks to cast a twelve-person play, rehearse a seventy-two-page script, and bring it to the Robert Moss theater ready to perform to a ninety-nine-seat theater. We would get three performances. Alice was quickly learning that I was a worrier, and around every turn she had me relax: no small task.

If Johnny Depp and Julie Andrews had a baby, you would get Alice. The quote by Coco Chanel that always makes me think of Maria now made me think of Alice: "Elegance comes from being as beautiful inside as outside."

———◆———

The first day of auditions didn't come without hitches. First, with Alice coming into the city from her friend's house in Prospect Park, Brooklyn, coupled with her still getting her subway bearings, she was almost an hour late. We had the room reserved for only four hours and had just one day to cast. The day felt rushed and unproductive. None of us felt we had found the best of the best. Most importantly, we hadn't secured a Maria. We needed a seventy-plus actor who could play elegant and edgy, charming and soulful and be able to keep long paragraphs of historical anecdotes compelling while also being able to sling pithy one-liners that made the audience roll with laughter. And she needed an Austrian accent that had to be distinct but understandable to a theater audience. We basically needed Vanessa Redgrave to walk through the door.

Toward the end of the day, on my way back to the room from getting a drink of water, I noticed a woman seated outside with shocking white hair, a la Meryl Streep in *The Devil Wears Prada*. I acknowledged her, went in the room, and sat back down next to Alice and Robin. We readied ourselves for the next actor. Robin's assistant Jess left the room and returned with Rochelle Slovin, the silver-haired woman from the hallway.

Rochelle began reading her lines with Jess. Her accent was perfect: decidedly Austrian yet altogether lucid. She was relaxed, showed strength but also sweetness, and never pushed anything too hard. I googled her as she auditioned. If what I was looking at in the search bar was the Rochelle Slovin we were looking at in front of us, she had founded and run the Museum of the Moving Image in Queens for thirty years, and was now, at age seventy-six, pursuing her second career as an actor.

Robin, Alice, and I sat at a café afterward, arranging the actors' headshots on a rickety, crumb-filled table. We mixed and matched the pictures and finally agreed on a cast. Robin hopped on the phone to alert the actors of the good news. We had exactly four weeks of rehearsals to get it ready. Later, Rochelle told us that she had never before attempted an Austrian accent and in fact was horrible at accents. She could have fooled us.

The rehearsal studio I booked was called The Producer's Club on Forty-Fourth and Ninth in Hell's Kitchen, which was about a twenty-minute walk east from Ruth's apartment. When I was in the market to purchase the space, the manager told me it was where Al Pacino used to rehearse. I met more than one person later who said: "Every rehearsal studio in Manhattan says that."

Very quickly, I learned to leave Alice alone in rehearsals. I was finding that in America, things were much less formal than in the UK. While in the States the playwright was usually at rehearsals, in the UK it was mostly the opposite. But it was complicated because I wasn't just the playwright; I was also the producer and the guy the story was about. Additionally, I was the guy footing the bill—all my own money. So I needed to be there. Alice respected that. After all, while the writer in the film world is considered second-rate to the director, in the theater world the playwright, not the director, is king. But there was no dispute who the king was here. It was the Boisterous Brit.

CHAPTER 29

Alice in Wonderland

Part Two

After four weeks of rehearsals, we weren't ready for an audience. We needed two more ... *years!* Rochelle wasn't completely off book—she still had some long, dense historical anecdotes to work out—the blocking needed futzing with, and our set designer was still finding and buying stage props. And then, on our opening night, January 26, 2015, a mammoth blizzard blasted Manhattan. At the last minute, the theater had to cancel our show. This sent a nihilistic shadow over the cast. Alice, who was always as cool as a cucumber, was devastated, which left me suicidal. *Would anyone show up now?*

But Maria and Gustav were watching through the glass wall.

The next evening, on our new opening night, with twelve inches of snow still on the ground, by some unexplainable miracle, every single seat was filled. They even had to add chairs to the front row to accommodate even more people than expected. The extra chairs were so close to the stage that the actors would have to work to avoid tripping over legs and feet during a scene.

Alice was originally planning not to attend opening night. She explained to me that UK theater directors generally don't attend out of respect for the actors. It's an old tradition. The performers worked hard for all those weeks, the show was as ready as it was going to get, and now seeing the director in the audience would basically translate into: our boss doesn't trust us.

But Alice broke tradition. She had come too far. She split the difference by sitting virtually unseen in the very back row. I was too nervous to be anywhere near the inside of the theater, so I spent every moment the play was running in the back hallway pacing like a tiger in its cage. Once in a while, I would hear an uproarious laugh, which made me walk farther out of earshot so I wouldn't jinx the next one. Sometimes I would hear a laugh at a line that was never laughed at in rehearsals. Those were the best.

At the end of the show, a towering man in a topcoat came right up to me and handed me his card. It said: *Georg Heindl, Austrian Consul General in New York*. Based on Maria's descriptions of Austrian politicians, along with my encounters with a few, I was thrown off a bit by Georg, because he wasn't stern, stoic, and unhelpful—he was warm, personable, and encouraging. He told me he enjoyed the play and that I should contact Christian Ebner at the Austrian Cultural Forum. With Georg being the first feedback I'd received, even before I had a chance to talk to Alice, I was living in a fantasy. We all celebrated at Brother Jim's on Eighth Avenue. We got free drinks because one of the cast members was a bartender there, so even my wallet was on cloud nine. The remaining two performances were sold out. Because it was a festival, they awarded prizes to the best three plays. Ours didn't win. But, of course, it did in our books.

Georg, only fifty-five, died suddenly in 2018. He was a lynchpin for the continued exposure of *The Accidental Caregiver* in New York, but what I'll most remember him for was how his heart lit up when he spoke.

CHAPTER 30

The Austrian Cultural Forum

Georg's colleague, Christian Ebner, the deputy director at the Austrian Cultural Forum New York, wanted me to put up the play as a staged reading, which meant the actors would be on stage acting everything out with scripts in hands. Instead of a cast of twelve, like at the Robert Moss, he wanted to make the play a two-hander—a play with two people. He wanted it to last no more than forty-five minutes and to be performed in June 2015.

It was February, and the script, as it was performed at the Robert Moss Theater, was seventy-two pages with a cast of twelve. I had four months to turn it into forty pages with a cast of two. Unfortunately, Alice left for the UK in January after our final show, so I tapped myself to direct. I got cooking on the script. They paid me rather well too, which almost never happens for a staged reading. This experience began a lasting relationship with the ACFNY. It meant a great deal to see that not all Austrian officials harbored ill will toward Maria; in fact, the people I met at the forum were eager to embrace the story.

I asked Rochelle to play Maria again—an honor she couldn't wait to revive—and an actor named Christian Scheider played yours truly. Christian is the son of the legendary actor Roy Scheider, one of my favorite actors of all time.

At the sold-out performance, I was delighted to see Stephen Lash, the chairman of Christie's, dressed in his impeccable three-piece suit I always told him he looked like he was born in. Out of all the elite "suits" involved in Maria's court case, Stephen and I connected the most over the years because we shared a similar love for Maria. I don't know what kind of relationship Stephen has or had with his own mother, but it always seemed like he treated Maria like his mother, and she him like her son. He had visited her in Cheviot Hills in 2011 hours before she passed. Seeing him surprise her at her bedside delighted her beyond words. She forgot all about her imminent death and became completely enthralled with the fact that Stephen had flown 3,000 miles just to say hello to her. Over the years, he's been one of my most ardent supporters.

After the performance at the forum, Stephen invited me to his office at the Christie's headquarters at Rockefeller Center. While sitting in his office, he said to me, "Gregor, I have a huge rolodex … Anyone you ever want to meet, just let me know." I have yet to take him up on it. That would be funny if he came to me one day and said, "Gregor, do you happen to know so-and-so?"

With all that was going on with the play, I still had a priority at home: Ruth. And getting her to leave her apartment was becoming more and more difficult. I could no longer just say, "Let's take a walk, Ruth." That revolutionary tactic wasn't working like it had two months prior. Lately, I had to think of an excuse, make up a story, or show her how her life would benefit from a walk. Usually, "There's an ice cream truck on the way," worked, and I would hope the one that was usually on the corner of Fortieth and Park didn't decide to take the day off. But sometimes not even ice cream would work, and I would have to tell Victoria that short of dragging her out by her arms her mother didn't get her walk.

Between the (lack of) walks, her continued avoidance of bathing, and being in the hospital every few weeks for urinary tract infections, it reminded me of the things that were happening to Maria just days before the end.

CHAPTER 31

Ruth

Part Two

New York is lonely.

New York is not lonely.

Here's what I mean:

New York is lonely in that you can walk out of your apartment at virtually any time of day or night and suddenly be in a sea of humans.

New York is not lonely in that you can walk out of your apartment at virtually any time of day or night and suddenly be in a sea of humans.

There's a lesser-known Mark Twain quote that comes to mind here: "New York is a splendid desert—a domed and steepled solitude, where the stranger is lonely in the midst of a million of his race."

My favorite pastime in New York, the thing that made me feel most alive, was walking Manhattan from tip to tip—from Ruth's at Thirty-Ninth Street over to Fifth Avenue, then up to One-Hundred and Tenth Street and Central Park East, then through the tippy top of the park (an area where I'd have to walk a little faster, if you know what I mean), then back down Central Park West all the way down to West Village, then east to Fourth Street, then up past Union Square, then Park Avenue back up to Thirty-Ninth. Sometimes I would trek twenty miles in one day. As I blew passed addresses, I couldn't help but think in wonderment: "Behind every address in New York is one hell of a story."

When I first moved in, Ruth and I spent a lot of time smiling at each other without much to say. I knew who she was, but I wasn't sure she knew who I was. I still couldn't quite believe I was in New York, and she probably couldn't quite believe she had a new roommate, which left us both in the same interesting boat trying to figure out exactly what our new lives meant. Ruth's innate reticence had me curious about what she really thought of me. She seemed content with the situation and with me, but there was also the possibility that she was hiding her discomfort, for example, seeing me walk out of my room in a T-shirt and shorts brushing my teeth. Was it okay? She never told me either way. Ruth's eternally congenial disposition and embrace of peaceful silences was one of the most therapeutic parts of my new life in New York.

Being the obsessive question-asker I am, I wanted to know everything about her life. Once I asked her what her favorite city was.

"New York," she answered immediately.

"Not Vienna?" I asked.

"That too," she said, and stared down at the table awkwardly. She had nothing left to say.

I eventually stopped asking questions entirely. I didn't want any tension between us. After all, in the short time I had been there, I knew her well enough not to need to ask anything. I even stopped asking her things like, "Would you like more apple juice?" I would just pour her a glass and put the container back in the fridge, and she would get more if she wanted. I was at peace with my role. If I made sure she had food in the fridge, that all the burners were turned off, and that we took our walks on Park Avenue down to at least Thirty-Sixth Street, our relationship didn't need to go deeper than that. Ruth was happy just seeing "the man she now lived with" sipping tea with her at the Scandinavia House across the street, or sitting at the kitchen table typing on his laptop while she sat in her comfy chair admiring her beach paintings.

While Ruth and I bonded almost exclusively without words, Maria and I bonded almost exclusively verbally, and most of our conversations were about her charmed childhood in Vienna. She had maintained an impeccable memory of her formative years that after seven decades still filled her with euphoria. The memories of her father, for example, always taking her to buy roasted chestnuts at the local park. And her governess Emma putting a live fish into the bathtub to swim around before cooking it for dinner. "I thought that was so gross," Maria would lament to me. "That was the bathtub I took baths in!"

One day I said to Ruth, "I want you to draw me." She wasn't interested until I brought her a pad and pencil and refused to budge until she got to work. She spent about five minutes on it. When she finished, she grew a devious grin and showed me what she sketched. I doubled over with laughter (It was me with a cartoon thought bubble containing a picture of a nude woman). It reminded me she was still sharp enough to know exactly what I would find funny. I told Victoria about it, and she said that Ruth had stopped drawing years ago. The vitality this one drawing seemed to give her, the sense of accomplishment that she visibly felt, probably added weeks to her life.

Ruth and I took regular walks to the Catholic Church on Park and Thirty-Eighth. Sometimes we'd enter a service already in progress; sometimes it was after hours, and we'd sit there in dusty silence, the faint sound of Midtown traffic mollifying us into meditation. Occasionally, the giant front doors would swing open, allowing the street sounds and whirling wind in, followed by chattering European tourists satisfying their church fetish. Ruth wasn't religious at all, but she loved that silent, dusty church.

Victoria would come over to the house once or twice a week for a sit-down dinner consisting mostly of some type of whitefish (hi Mom), fresh coleslaw, and a sweet potato from D'Agostino's. Because Victoria lived all the way on Roosevelt Island and had her own life across the pond, visiting her mom hadn't become as regular as it should have been. Now that I was breathing new life into Ruth's final days, Victoria wanted to be around to see that. Seeing this positive affect I was having on Ruth's family brought me the feelings of familial belonging I always sought.

One time, in the middle of the night, I was having the most incredible dream. I was in my room enjoying the most intoxicating smell of toast coming from the kitchen. I couldn't wait to wake up and eat this toast, so I opened my eyes, ready to get out of bed and enjoy it. As I got my bearings, I noted a faint plume of smoke collecting under the door. *Wow,* I thought, *Someone is really cooking up a masterpiece this morning! I should go tell Ruth.*

Suddenly, I leapt out of my bed, ran into the kitchen, and found a pot, once shiny and silver, burnt to a crisp, the stovetop fire still blazing. Inside the pot was a piece of charcoal I deduced at one time had been an egg. I turned off the burner, ran the pot under cold water, and threw it out. I was certain that if I had slept another few minutes, Ruth and I would have been … toast. I leaned into Ruth's room—she was fast asleep. I chuckled at her serene expression, not a care in the world.

Victoria maintained that her mother's memory loss was due to being a normal ninety-seven-year-old. She didn't believe it was Alzheimer's. From my perspective, it doesn't even matter. I do know that the common belief was that Maria developed dementia towards the end and in those final days, if I left the room and returned five minutes later, she would greet me as if she hadn't seen me in days. Ruth never had this issue. Chuck always bragged about Maria's memory, saying that in her prime she could name all five hundred of her clothing clients by first and last name.

There's the obvious downside to what the medical world calls Alzheimer's and dementia, especially as it pertains to loved ones having to watch it get worse, but with Maria I always chose to focus on the upsides of it—that they have little to no awareness of it. They live nearly every moment of their day in the present. And at least the disorder itself doesn't cause physical pain. Focusing on their light rather than their decline made Maria's final days the best they could be.

Perhaps the more salient issue is why the medical community seems to spend so much time on the wrong thing. I attended an Alzheimer's convention in 2017 in New York, and the main event consisted of doctors giving PowerPoint presentations about how little they knew of the cause and the cure. Not that it was all futile, and not that they weren't earnest, but was it really productive? Was it magically making grandchildren care more about grandparents? Regardless, most medical professionals agree that the most effective current "cure" for Alzheimer's and dementia is to keep the mind as stimulated as possible. Sometimes the best thing you can do, like I did often with Maria, is, for example, play a game of Scrabble. With Ruth, drawing that picture of me brought her purpose, and longevity.

Ruth died on October 11, 2015, at age ninety-seven. I was out that day and had learned that Alexandra and Victoria were with her and noticed she was having trouble breathing. They took her to the hospital. It was congestive heart failure. Victoria thought it best not to visit her. She was gone three days later. It reminded me of Edith, Maria's friend from high school. She was one of the most healthy-seeming ninety-year-olds I had ever met. Whenever she visited Maria's she always drifted through the front door with endless supplies of energy and optimism. One day we heard she was taken to the hospital. A week later she was gone. Maria didn't even have a chance to say goodbye. It all happens so quickly in your nineties.

Alexandra was hit the hardest. She adored her grandmother, and they shared a very close bond. Alexa couldn't bear setting foot in the house anymore or even wear any of Ruth's clothes she inherited. Though Ruth spent most of her time in her comfy chair in a meditative state, the apartment somehow suddenly felt sucked of energy. Victoria and I spent the next few weeks gutting the place, taking out all the books, the designer outfits, the paintings—it was a daunting task. To this day, we're trying to figure out a way to show Ruth's paintings to the public. As I said, there are around four hundred. Her best of the best are stunning. Ruth's use of white tape on some of her wilderness works is singular. I wrote up Ruth Rogers-Altmann's Wikipedia page. Read more there about her fascinating life in art and fashion, and feel free to add to it.

We had a memorial service at 71 Park with her closest friends. Jose, the building handyman, was there. When Ruth moved into the apartment in the 1960s, a young Jose had just gotten a job as a doorman. Their friendship had lasted nearly half a century.

One of the attendees was an eighty-eight-year-old French painter named Nicole Bigar who I was meeting for the first time. She was Ruth's closest friend. They had met in the 1990's in the Hamptons at the Art Barge, which is a World War II ship turned into an art studio in 1960 by Victor D'Amico, the Director of the Department of Education at the Museum of Modern Art in New York. Nicole and Ruth took art classes there together. "In class I kept noticing how old her art supplies were," Nicole said, her eyes sparkling in remembrance. "So one day I brought her new supplies and from then on we were good friends."

Over the next few weeks, Nicole and I would go to the opera together, she would come see a play I wrote at the Manhattan Repertory Theater on Forty-Second (a really dark and irreverent one, which I'm sure wasn't her favorite), and we would take strolls in Central Park across the street from her apartment on Fifth Avenue at Ninety-Second Street, just two blocks from the Guggenheim Museum. My presence reminded her of Ruth and how she was well taken care of in her final days. One time on a walk I was wearing shorts and a T-shirt and Nicole noticed my two tattoos—the gold portrait on my right calf and a Rothko on my left arm.

"My goodness," she exclaimed, stopping in her tracks staring at my bare limbs. "Your body is a canvas!"

My canvas ended up spending the summer of 2018 with Nicole at her beachfront house in East Hampton, by Georgica Pond, where

I wrote a significant portion of this book. Virtually every day we hung out at the Art Barge. While Nicole was in her element painting and sculpting inside the ship, I was outside on the deck, laptop open, watching the passing birds and windsurfers.

Nicole lived in the most exclusive area of East Hampton. To give you an idea, her neighbor was Calvin Klein's wife ... about ten houses down the street was Steven Spielberg ... on the adjacent street was Martha Stewart ... and across the street from Spielberg was the famous *Grey Gardens* house, from the documentary of the same name.

This was absolute paradise in my book. During the day, wild rabbits hopped through Nicole's front lawn, and there was a revolving door of deer dashing just about everywhere we went. There was a deer population problem in the Hamptons. The poor babies had nowhere to go, so they were forced to set up shop in resident's yards.

At night, there were no streetlights on Nicole's part of the road. When the sun went down, it got so dark that walking outside was like feeling your way around a windowless room in the middle of the night.

CHAPTER 32

A Woman

GREGOR. It's official. I can't find a woman.

MARIA. What happened, my love?

GREGOR. Don't you see everything I do?

MARIA. Only when I ask Gustav to take me to the room. But that wouldn't be fair to you—to spy on you all the time. Plus, I might get jealous.

GREGOR. Maria. A woman is aaaaaalways a woman.

MARIA. You said that very dramatically, just like Plácido said it!

GREGOR. I wasn't going to tell you, but Plácido just got accused of sexual harassment. It was all over the news. It's this whole #MeToo movement.

MARIA. Me too?

GREGOR. Forget it. You weren't around to see it. Probably a good thing.

MARIA. Well, I'm not surprised. Plácido was always into women. You know, his first job was at a Mexican bordello. He was hired as the piano player.

GREGOR. Right. And he was paid in the form of … you know.

MARIA. Did I tell you that?

GREGOR. Of course. Anyway, Europe is fighting back. They love Plácido. Americans are too uptight about everything.

MARIA. I find it hard to believe.

GREGOR. Americans are totally uptight when it comes to sex.

MARIA. No, that you can't find a woman.

GREGOR. It's true.

MARIA. You just don't want to find one.

GREGOR. I'm too independent.

MARIA. Darling.

GREGOR. Ever since I met you, I'm more and more down the dark hole of independence. You glorified me too much. Held me in too high esteem. It's like no girl I meet measures up.

MARIA. It's not that they don't measure up. It's that you don't think you measure up. Stop using me as an excuse.

GREGOR. Why was I so deeply into you?

MARIA. Because I showed up and loved you like a woman should love you. I loved you for you. You need a woman who can love you like that. Life isn't perfect, my love, but it's wonderful.

CHAPTER 33

Soul Mates

This is an excerpt from *The Accidental Caregiver* stage play, directed by Alice Kornitzer and premiered at the Robert Moss Theater on January 26, 2015 (under twelve inches of snow). Grant is Gregor and Ed is Tom, the guy who got me the job caring for Maria. Russell is a character loosely based on a few friends I have in Los Angeles.

———————◆◆———————

Russell and Grant are in a dingy bar.

GRANT. Russell.

RUSSELL. Russell's dead. He got dragged into a ditch by a polar bear.

GRANT. He was my friend.

RUSSELL. The polar bear?

GRANT. Furry little thing.

RUSSELL. What did you want, by the way?

GRANT. Nothing. Forget it.

RUSSELL. Dude, I haven't seen you guys in forever! What's up with Ed and that whole bungalow business?

GRANT. The family's still looking for a caregiver. Whatever. I don't know if I want to do it.

RUSSELL. What's with this caregiving epidemic all of a sudden? You and Ed are making me look like a schmuck! And my aunt. The whole world's getting sick.

GRANT. I don't hear much about your aunt.

RUSSELL. Aunt Murphy. She's going deaf, blind, and they said something about her becoming demented.

GRANT. She probably has dementia.

RUSSELL. Look at you, Mr. Caregiver. She's only seventy. God, that's young!

GRANT. She close?

RUSSELL. To death? Jesus, Grant! Now I gotta take a shot.

GRANT. Proximity-wise, you moron.

RUSSELL. Oh. San Diego. She's gonna need someone. Fucking Father Time!

GRANT. Hey, what's your take on soul mates?

RUSSELL. They're great.

GRANT. They can be anyone, right? Any two people. Any age, race, whatever. And it doesn't have to be a sexual thing, or if it's sexual, then it can be something you both know is there and can enjoy without the pressure or desire to act on it.

RUSSELL. Are you having some weird fling with that old lady?

GRANT, *playing it off.* What? No, but I met a girl. At the gym. Jessica. I don't want to have sex with her. I just want to be around her. It's weird.

RUSSELL. I had this hamster growing up—speaking of soul mates—that I swear could like read my mind. He would stare right into my eyes. Not in a gay way. It was like he was a … spirit.

GRANT. You mean like a ghost?

RUSSELL. A spirit.

GRANT. A kindred spirit.

RUSSELL. Sort of. Yeah. I always wonder if I saw him today if he'd still recognize me or … see me. Like really see me.

GRANT. We'll never know. I got acting class. Peace.

Grant leaves Russell with his beer.

CHAPTER 34

The Ditty of Brotherly Love

In late 2010, a few weeks before Maria died, she and I were in the thick of one of our usual undulating conversations on her back terrace, topics ranging from acting to art to music to women. At one point, she said to me, "Darling, I'm going to be looking down on you for the rest of your life to make sure you find the right woman." Finding the right woman hasn't happened yet, but if Maria was watching me through that glass wall during the week of September 3, 2018, she would have watched four women in a seven-day period break their plans with me.

Little did I know at the time, this 168-hour stretch would end up putting into check a belief system I had cemented in my brain for much of my adult life. So I have Brie, Maybeline, Alexandria, and Kalina to thank for a breakthrough with my brother Christian.

Brie (Monday, August 18, 2018)

The week began with my plans with Brie. I met her on Bumble, a dating app where the woman has to make the first move. The way it works is, once you match up—i.e., you have both swiped right on each other—the woman has twenty-four hours to send you a message, or the match dissolves forever. Brie, like the noble woman she seemed to be in that early stage, said hello in the twenty-four-hour window, and we quickly moved the conversation to text. She was a tall, attractive black and Indian girl who, based on our text messages, was also intelligent and playful.

When I mentioned I was a writer and somewhat of a grammarian (although my editor might disagree), she became self-conscious, apologizing in advance for insulting my scholastic sensibilities with her texts. We found this back-and-forth endearing, and I'd playfully scold her if I received any texts that appeared to be written by a third grader. This intellectual tennis match went on for a couple days, and we decided to make plans for the coming Monday.

We were going to meet at Columbus Circle at eleven o'clock in the morning at the entrance to Central Park on Fifty-Eighth and Eighth. I lived within walking distance, so I left my apartment around 10:45, walking at a leisurely pace. Halfway there, I got a text: "Got called into work last minute, I'm so sorry. Let's reschedule." This surprised but hardly bothered me, having no idea of the week ahead of me. Her excuse note was written with flawless grammar, so I gave her a pass. I turned around and went to Planet Fitness on Fifty-Fifth. We never spoke again.

Maybeline (Wednesday, August 20, 2018)

Tuesday evening I was meeting my friend Andrea at a bar in Soho for a going-away party for one of her friends. I was early, so I stopped into an Italian eatery down the street to grab a snack before heading to the bar. As I stood at the entryway skeptically reading the menu, a sprightly Latin girl with flowing brown hair and sporting a baseball cap so low her ears jutted out like Dumbo encouraged me to come in and order. *Well now I have to eat here.*

I walked to the counter where another cute girl took my order. I found a seat. The Latin girl kept side-eyeing me as I waited for my food. It wasn't a surprise when the food came to my table and she was carrying it. After we exchanged side-eyes, I dug in to the pasta. At one point I realized I didn't have a napkin, and as if she read my mind, she showed up with a handful of napkins. I found her bold flirtations refreshing. I wasn't used to girls half my age being this clear about what they wanted.

On one of her walks past my table, I summoned her over with a smile and a slight lift of the chin. This seemed to surprise her. I got the feeling she wasn't used to "old" white guys showing initiative. "We may as well just exchange numbers," I suggested, both of us quickly pulling out our phones in agreement. I left with an extra pep in my step and met Andrea at the bar.

Maybeline and I agreed to meet the next day. The plan was that I'd return to the restaurant as her shift was ending, and we'd walk to Washington Square Park where sitting on a bench people-watching could take up half a day. She got off at six, so I headed down there and walked into the restaurant. She was behind the desk, still dressed in her work clothes, rolling her eyes.

"I'm so sorry. My boss is saying I need to work more. Can I take a rain check?"

I asked her why she didn't tell me earlier, before I went through the trouble of getting on a train all the way down, but she blew it off, and when she blew that off, she started to act her age, which turned me off completely. I was dealing with a child. Whatever.

Alexandria (Friday, August 22, 2018)

I met Alexandria on Bumble. She was thirty-seven, Columbian and Puerto Rican, and had a five-year-old daughter. After dealing with someone half my age, Alexandria presented the stability I needed. We set a date to meet at the Sailboat Pond in Central Park at Seventy-Second Street at one o'clock in the afternoon. I told her to meet me right by "that statue with the ducks." When I showed up, no one was there. At 1:10, I texted her: "I'm here, are you en route?" Nothing. I got really pissed. *What is going on with humans in my life?*

Halfway home, I got a text: "You're going to kill me but I was out late and slept late and just got up. Plus I didn't think you'd really show up anyway."

I texted back: "Let me know how assuming someone won't keep their word works out for you in the future." When I got home, I texted her back: "I'm sorry. I've just been flaked on a lot this week. Let's get together some other time."

She texted back: "That was big of you. Impressed, party of one."

We tentatively set a date, but it didn't really feel that genuine. Next.

Kalina (Saturday, August 24, 2018)

I was batting zero, and I had one more chance to crawl out from under the rock. Kalina felt like the one. It was another dating-app meeting, but we never actually met. Way back in May 2018, we went from Bumble to phone to WhatsApp to FaceTime. This was important—that we saw each other in full motion.

Kalina was a flight attendant for a private airline catering to upscale clientele. At a moment's notice, she would have to jump on a plane and fly somewhere. This seemed like a high-profile job that required reliability and professionalism. I liked that. And her whisking away at a moment's notice didn't scare me. It appealed to me. It showed me she was independent and curious. I wasn't looking for a smotherer or for someone to complete me, just someone I could spend time with and have fun things to talk about—it worked for Maria and me.

While I spent the summer of 2018 in the Hamptons with Nicole, Kalina and I spoke a few times a week. We tried to figure out a time and a place to meet, which depended on her flying schedule, but it never quite worked out.

Finally we set a date for September 8 at eleven o'clock in the morning at the Jackie Onassis Reservoir, near Nicole's Upper East Side apartment. Can you tell I like meeting dates at Central Park? Like the pathetic shithead I am, I showed up on time and waited until 11:30

before giving up. And she never got back to me. She may as well have never existed.

The universe had gone over the line. I called my friend Greg, a television producer in Los Angeles. We had started out together on the television show *Blind Date* back in 1999, he as an executive assistant and me as a tape librarian. While I eventually quit reality television, he stuck with it, and is now a successful television executive. He offered some good old-fashioned wisdom. "Everyone goes through tough stretches. It doesn't have anything to do with you. Keep your head up." The advice didn't hurt, but I was still upset.

I don't usually call my mom with women problems, but I was running out of ideas. During our talk, she was positive, but I didn't need positivity. I needed honesty. We didn't really get anywhere. I had called her in a depressed state, and I hung up that way.

That night before bed, my phone rang. It was my brother. Because my phone saying "Christian" was an extremely rare thing, it suddenly hit me that my mom must have told him to check in on me. Why else would I be hearing from him? I didn't answer. He called three more times. I let them all go to voicemail. Then he texted. *Five times.* Christian hadn't texted me five times in one whole year, and here he was doing it in one night. I didn't respond.

The next morning I woke up to about twelve texts. I was convinced what I was going through was way too complicated for him to understand, but I called him anyway.

Ten minutes later, I had a new outlook on two things: life, and my brother. He suggested I get into a daily routine. Get up early, work out, stay active. I hadn't been in a relationship for a long time, big deal he said, I just needed to get back into practice. Go on some dates, be social, get the mojo back. He was logical, understanding, and nonjudgmental—all things I spent much of my adult life not giving him credit for. I could feel my world opening up because I was opening up.

The next day, Sunday, September 4, 2018, I tuned in to the US

Open Tennis Championship match between Rafael Nadal and Dominic Thiem. It went to a fifth set tiebreaker. Nadal won. For some reason, I was so moved by Thiem's performance, and, him being Austrian, I couldn't help but think of Maria up there watching on the glass wall. I texted Guenter about it. (You remember Guenter from part one, I had met him on my Golden Trip to Austria, and we've been close friends ever since.) I don't know why, but the match spoke to the deepest part of me. Seeing the raw passion in Nadal and Thiem sparked in me a kind of renewal. I felt even closer to Christian.

Life is like Michael Douglas or the amount of time it takes me to eat a powdered donut: short.

CHAPTER 35

Humans in My Phone

It was early December 2018 when I stood in line at my dry cleaners clenching a couple button-downs watching Jay of Jay Cleaners display his usual Maria Altmann joie de vivre with his customers. As I stepped to the counter and set my shirts free, I pulled out my iPhone and told him I wanted to film him with it. He was sure I was kidding and then just plum crazy, insisting, "I'm so boring!" He eventually came around.

I went straight to B&H Photo on Thirty-Fourth, bought a Rode directional mic that pops right into the iPhone, and returned at ten o'clock the next morning to spend about thirty minutes recording him *doing his thing*. After that, I rushed home, imported the footage into iMovie, cut it to ninety seconds, returned to Jay's an hour later with my laptop, and clicked play for him. A grin began forming, his face began reddening, and before the video even ended, he gave me a high-five and went back to work.

This sparked an idea.

In my itinerate life of work and play, my unending curiosity has led me to an eclectic blend of friends all over the world, living the creative life. So what was I waiting for? I started going through my phone and texting all my artistic peeps in New York: "I just launched this micro-doc series I want to include you in. You free Friday at 2?" Soon, I was meeting with two or three in a week. As of December 2019, I've shot one hundred of them. The series is titled *Humans in My Phone* (*HIMP* for short), and I shoot them mostly in New York and Los Angeles.

My shoots aren't willy-nilly. I have rules. One is, your number has to already be in my phone. Another is that the videos don't exceed sixty seconds. They're all linked to YouTube and are meant to be merely a taste of a life. Under each video is a link to learn more about the subject. I even made one of Maria. I took some old footage of us and edited together a sixty-second piece where I tell a funny story.

I feel like a portrait painter with a phone. Like a painter, I convey my subjects as they are, using natural light, and through shot selection and editing, I get to add my own pathos. Three cool things happened right away. One subject I shot, a songwriter friend of mine named Betty, was contacted by a music producer from Sweden who wanted to work with her after seeing her video. Second, I was solicited to teach a How to Shoot Micro-Docs class, which I taught at the People's Improv Theater during the spring of 2019. And lastly, Trina Wyatt, cofounder of the Tribeca Film Festival with Robert De Niro, launched a website called Conscious Good and wants me to run some workshops to teach high school kids how to use their phones to tell stories.

Aside from being fun and creatively stimulating, *HIMP* has also been a great way to reconnect with old friends. At least two dozen subjects are good friends I hadn't seen in months, and their shoot served not only to immortalize their creative spirits but also to have a pretty damn good excuse to catch up.

HIMP involves everyone from dry cleaners to painters to chairmen to Holocaust survivors—all friends who are creatively impacting the world in some way. One of my subjects, an actor-director friend named Winsome, called the videos "like poems." I'd like to think they're odes to the creative life, to that relentless search for truth and tranquility through human connection; they show independent and established artists on equal footing, daily pursuing their passions with unending drive, often choosing creation and exploration over peace and comfort.

I think of the accidental creative path I've been on since meeting Maria in 2008. Maybe it will be written on my headstone one day: *Introducing the world to the people in his life.*

CHAPTER 36

Death Scene

This is how I wrote Maria's death scene in *The Accidental Caregiver* stage play. Though the setting and placement of the dialogue are constructed specifically for the script, the words we said to each other, especially in the moments leading up to her death, are verbatim. Those final words we traded—about "packing for Vienna"—still play in my head.

———◆———

GRANT. Oh, I have a joke for you! Well I'm borrowing it from the nurse. So … a guy in a convertible is driving with a pig in the passenger seat. A cop pulls him over and says, "Sir, you can't drive around with a pig, you need to bring him to the zoo." The guy says okay. Next day he's driving with his pig again, and the same cop pulls him over. "Sir, I thought I told you to take him to the zoo." Guy says, "I did. Then I took him to the movies."

Maria giggles weakly.

MARIA. Grant?
GRANT. Yes?

MARIA. Do you know that I'm going to be up there looking down on you for the rest of your life?

GRANT. Yeah. Okay.

MARIA. That I'll be making sure you find the woman of your dreams, that everyone is good to you, and that you achieve everything you ever wanted in life?

GRANT. We don't have to get into this right now.

MARIA. Do you know that I'll be with you forever?

He can't contain it any longer.

GRANT. Why did we have to meet?

MARIA. Mein Schatz.

GRANT. It's not fair! Why couldn't we have met in another life when we were young? There's no justice! I finally meet the woman … who I can talk to … who understands me … why can't we be together forever? Why can't love stop death?

MARIA. You made the last three years of my life worth living.

He lies his head on her bosom; she strokes his hair.

GRANT. I don't know what I'm supposed to do anymore.

MARIA. Listen to me, darling. All that you'll ever need in life is already within you.

GRANT. All I want is to be here with you.

MARIA, *with a sudden fear.* I don't want to close my eyes.

GRANT, *lifting his head up.* Why don't you want to close your eyes?

MARIA. Because I may never see you again.

GRANT. I'm finding a doctor. I'm calling Ed.

MARIA. Don't leave me. Help me stay awake. Please.

GRANT. I'm here. I'm not leaving ever again. I love you so much.

MARIA. I have something for you.

She gives him a small box.

GRANT. Can I open it?

MARIA. Later. (*She looks at him.*) Mein Schatz?

GRANT. Yes?

MARIA. Did you pack?

GRANT. Did I pack? For Vienna? Of course I packed. I got our plane tickets all ready. The taxi is out front. Are you ready?

MARIA. I'M READY.

She squeezes his hand.

She's gone.

Lights go dark.

A gorgeous silence.

CHAPTER 37

Beatdown

On Friday, June 1, 2018, at around nine thirty in the evening, I was minding my business walking home up the east side of Ninth Avenue just about to reach Forty-Second Street—when I felt something bump my left shoulder. I had just hoofed it thirty-three blocks from Father Demo Square in West Village, where I had been with my friend Meng, seated on our usual bench facing the exceedingly overrated Joe's Pizza on Carmine Street in the throes of one of our classic back-and-forths about how awake we were and how asleep the world was.

Since at this time of night sidewalks were littered with flesh, brushing against another body was inevitable, especially on this stretch in Hell's Kitchen where the sidewalks are barely wide enough for three people to walk side by side. I thought little of the bump until I heard a "Yo!" shouted from behind me.

I turned my head. Through the hustle and bustle of tourists, a man was stopped dead, his eyes trained right on me. I waved an apology from the distance, continuing on my way. "Don't walk away from me!" shouted the irate man.

I stopped, turned back around, and waited for him to make his way to my face.

"Why you playin' wit me like that?" he asked.

I rolled my eyes and turned to leave. But as I stepped, he stepped. Unless I wanted to bring him home with me for dinner, I had to stop and deal with him.

But before we could do that, two other guys materialized, each stopping on one side of the shoulder-bumper. *Shoulder-bumper has coworkers.* My stomach sank into my toes. Survival mode took over. I knew right then that my only chance of getting home was to apologize more than I had ever apologized before.

Shoulder-bumper responded to my apologies: "You ain't goin' nowhere till you pay me a toll."

I made it clear to him that he wasn't being fair, and that I had already apologized to him and that should have been enough. The three tightened the gap between us. It was getting into smelling-everyone's-breath time.

I looked to his two footmen for a glimpse of humanity. One of them I could tell had a soft spot. I looked into his eyes with a knowing compassion. He looked away in shame. But he wasn't going to fold.

That's when the punches rained. The first was thrown by the shoulder-bumper—he clocked me square in the jaw. Then the footmen followed his lead, their flurry of fists forcing me against the wall of a deli. I was so in shock that I didn't even think to run away. I could have gone into the crowds and lost them. But I took the punches like my feet were super glued to the concrete. I sprinted into a 99-cent Pizza store at the corner. This was my refuge. Someone would call the cops.

When I barreled into the store, there were no customers, just two pizza guys behind the counter staring back at me like, "Are you getting a slice or not?" I told them I was assaulted and asked them to call the police. They heard me, they understood me, but they weren't going to do anything for me. Suddenly, the three thugs swung open the doors, the shoulder-bumper clutching a bottle. The pizza guys backed away from the counter, one ducking behind an oven. I couldn't blame them. How many fights had they seen this week? I was probably one of dozens.

The next thing I knew, a bottle was crashing over my head. Then a trash can, then a twelve-pack of sodas, all hurled at me. If it wasn't nailed down, it was thrown. The store went into chaos. At one point, I felt a hand slip into my pocket. Moments later it ripped open, my wallet and credit cards spraying onto the floor. It was a mad dash for plastic. I kept feeling my backpack over my shoulders being tugged, which had my laptop, and my unfinished manuscript. One of them was determined to get my bag. I held onto it like I was holding onto my soul. They would have had to pry it out of my dead hands. The credit cards I didn't care about. I could cancel them.

After what felt like an hour into the beatdown, as far as I could tell, no one ogling at the fight through the window had called the cops or done anything to help.

It was just another video they couldn't wait to post to Instagram.

This is when a fourth man showed up, only he wasn't trying to get in a punch; he was there to help. I later told the cops and lawyers he was the "Good Samaritan." He started shielding me from the punches and screaming at the guys, "Stop it, man! He didn't do anything!"

I kept thinking, *How did he know I didn't start the fight?* The three continued their barrage of beatdowns, now having extra bones to punch through to get to mine. *Why are they still beating me?* That was the real question I kept asking myself. They already had my wallet. They had what they came for. There was only one logical answer—they weren't out for money; they were out for blood.

Because the Good Samaritan and I were doing a pretty good job batting away the fists and objects being flung at me, the men finally relented and strolled out of the store as if nothing happened. I asked the Samaritan—Chante was his name—if he called the cops, and he said his girlfriend, who was outside the store, did. Nearly eight minutes (the amount of time I later learned had elapsed) had gone by since the first punch was thrown out on the sidewalk, in the heart of the most famous city in the world, where there was not one police officer in sight.

I was bleeding from head to toe. The crashing bottle had opened a gaping wound on the left side of my head, and it seemed to be spouting fresh blood by the second. I pulled out my phone to make sure the cops were on their way. But my hands were so bloody my screen wouldn't respond to touch. And I couldn't wipe the phone on my shirt because it was just as bloody.

"Can someone get me a napkin or something?" I called out. Moments later a paper napkin was thrust in my face. I wiped my fingers and phone screen, dialed 9-1-1, and connected to the dispatch. I started telling them what happened when I heard an ambulance siren in the distance. "They're here. I have to go," I said and hung up.

Chante stayed by my side even after the cops showed up. *Why didn't I throw any counter punches?* I kept asking myself. I didn't know. I just kept telling myself "keep blocking their punches until they decide to leave." Chante and I exchanged numbers. I promised I'd call him to thank him more when I had time to make sense of it all. He probably saved my life.

The ambulance arrived, and I sat in the back as they wrapped my head in gauze. A detective popped his head in to ask if I remembered what the suspects were wearing, and where they went. I remembered the shoulder-bumper was wearing a gray hoodie, and one of them was wearing a dark jacket. But I had no idea where they went.

I was driven to Mt. Sinai on Fifty-Ninth and Tenth, and just as I was being wheeled into the hospital, two cops ran in to tell me they had three suspects in custody somewhere around Thirty-Seventh and Tenth. They needed me to ID them. I was escorted into the back of a squad car.

"When we pull up," one of the officers said, "just peek through the crack in the window and tell us if we have the right guys, okay?"

When we arrived at the scene, I peered through the crack. Four or five police officers surrounded three cuffed men in front of an old, abandoned building on Tenth. It was them. There was no doubt in my mind.

The coworkers were calm, but the shoulder-bumper was seething with anger, spitting on any cop who got too close. Here was a guy who had intentionally bumped my shoulder so he could force me to pay him a toll, pummeled me for nearly ten minutes, pocketed my credit cards, and was now standing on a street corner threatening to kill anyone who disapproved of what he did. Later I asked one of the officers about some of the things he was yelling.

"He kept saying he was going to give us all a dirt nap," the officer said.

"What's a dirt nap?" I asked naively.

"Kill us and bury us in the dirt," he said. "It's an old mafia thing."

I was driven back to the hospital, given six giant stitches, and released around three o'clock in the morning.

It felt surreal being engulfed by mobs of people all night and then suddenly walking home alone in spooky silence with a fresh head wound. Questions filled my mind. Why didn't I run? Should I have paid the toll? Did I somehow attract this? Where the hell were the cops? While I sat on the hospital bed earlier getting stitched up, to explain why there weren't any officers around, one officer stated that it happened during a shift change. "Horrible luck, man," he said, shaking his head.

Even if he was covering something up, my conflicted views of law enforcement before the incident had undergone a deep-tissue massage. Throughout the entire ordeal, I felt taken care of. They definitely needed to clean up Port Authority and they needed more police presence there, but that was more a Mayor Bill de Blasio matter than a police matter. The whole incident proved that anything could happen to anyone at any time in any place.

It turns out it was all caught on camera. All the punches, the bottle smash, the trash can, the twelve-pack of sodas, Chante The Good Samaritan—every second would be seen by cops, lawyers, a jury, and a judge. The suspects had zero chance of getting off. It was an open-and-shut case.

Yet all three attackers pled not guilty. We were going to trial. They were career criminals with nothing to lose. To justify their gang assault, the shoulder-bumper told his lawyer I called him the N-word and spat in his face. It didn't matter that it was untrue; the claim was on public records, and the jury would hear it. I was assigned a district attorney who worked with the defense attorney to set a court date. When the first date came, an attorney got sick, and they had to postpone it. The next date was set for July 2018, but when the time came, it was postponed again for God knows what.

I needed a vacation.

CHAPTER 38

Vacation

July 2019 came, and after two or three more postponements, there was still no court date. It had been a creatively unproductive last few weeks for me, and I was determined to get out of New York for the sweaty months. I was so committed to my furlough that, before I had a clue where I'd go or what I'd do, I sent out a mass text saying I was subletting my Hell's Kitchen apartment from July 15 to September 1. That would also give me enough time to finish the book.

My friend Dana Barron was the first to reply to my sublet text—I'll get to how her reply fits into the fabric in a moment. But first, I'd like to tell you who she is. For anyone older than forty, Dana played Audrey in the eighties movie *Vacation* starring Chevy Chase. We met at the hair salon of my friend and former neighbor Shann Christen in Los Angeles in 2010.

The day we met, as Shann was cutting my hair, I looked at the next chair over.

"I think I know that girl," I whispered to Shann.

"A lot of people say that," he smirked.

"What do you mean?"

"That's Audrey from *Vacation*."

No wonder I thought I knew her. Vacation was one of my all-time favorite movies. I'd seen it at least a hundred times. If John Hughes movies helped define the eighties in a dramatic way, the *Vacation* movies helped define them in a comedic way. Dana still looked as cute as she did when she was a sixteen-year-old kid road-tripping across America with a giant

Panavision camera in her face. When my hair was finished, I swiveled in my chair while Shann's assistant finished up Dana's color.

We chatted for a long time. I never brought up the movie, in fact I don't think Dana even knew that I knew who she was. We were just two people talking about life. That same afternoon we went to a movie at the Westside Pavilion down the street, which has since been turned into six hundred square feet of Google offices. To this day, neither of us can remember what movie we saw.

So back to 2019 and Dana's text: She had an old friend named Paul who was interested in subletting the apartment for the forty-five day hiatus. After a five-minute phone call, Paul was on board. Now I could plan my trip. I decided I'd visit old friends in Los Angeles, go to Brazil—a country I had dreamed of visiting for a long time—and then figure it out from there.

That's when I heard back from Jamie, the district attorney in the beatdown case. They finally had a date she promised was set in stone this time: the week of July 15. *Uh-oh.* That was the day Paul was scheduled to move in, and the day I officially had nowhere to stay in New York. I lamented to Jamie that for more than a year they had pulled me in different directions, and now it was my turn for scheduling payback. I said I wanted out entirely. I had gone from, "I want those guys to rot in hell," to, "I hope they don't know where I live," to, "I just want there to be more police officers in that area." I had lost all passion for justice. And what was I going to do in court? Sit there and try and convince everyone I didn't call the shoulder-bumper the N-word? That I wasn't a racist? No thanks. But Jamie insisted that it was my duty to testify. She would do anything for me to be there, even put me up in a hotel for the week. Later that day she confirmed a hotel. I was impressed.

I planned my trip. I'd stay in my court-appointed hotel for the trial week, then I'd stay with Dana in LA for a week, then I'd go to Rio for a week, then San Francisco to visit my brother, then Long Beach Island to visit my friend Daniel, then Jersey City to visit my friend Dean, then back in my apartment September 1 and get the book to my editor Jessica by September 15. But as this was solidifying, Dana texted me to say I couldn't stay at her place until August 1. So I was left with eleven days after my court-appointed hotel with nowhere to sleep.

And where was I going to sleep for those eleven days, dear reader? I had an idea.

But to fully appreciate the idea, we have to rewind to January 2018. And before we even do that, come to Mexico with Maria and me!

CHAPTER 39

The Accidental Caregiver ... Mexico?

For being one of the top 50 Fixed Index Annuity producers at her company, in October 2017, they invited my mom to a vacation retreat in Cancún. After they solidified the itinerary, purchased the hundreds of flights, reserved airport shuttles, and booked hotel rooms, the US government spoke up—don't travel to Mexico. There was an uptick in kidnappings and murders. The company decided not to risk it and pulled out, losing hundreds of thousands of dollars. They changed the destination to a resort in Phoenix. My mom, given a plus-one, invited me. The weekend was set for May 2018.

Mexico hadn't panned out for my mom's retreat, but it would soon circle back in a big way.

I spent most of the weekend lounging on plastic patio furniture sipping florescent blue drinks with perfectly square ice cubes watching my mom fielding hugs and high-fives from swaths of burly, beer-gutted forty-something frat boys like they were on Spring Break. At seventy-two, my mom was the second oldest producer at a company of about 300. She had a stellar sales year. I was so proud of her.

One afternoon hanging around the pool, I got to talking to a woman named Claudia, an independent event planner working with the company. We hit it off at first sentence. Naturally, the topic of Maria and the paintings arose, and Claudia was delighted to share that she had just seen the movie *Woman in Gold*. She told me she lived in a pueblo in Mexico called San Miguel de Allende, where there was a really cool art scene and a surprisingly large Jewish community. Without much seriousness, she said, "Maybe you could come down someday with your book." *Wouldn't that be nice.* We exchanged emails.

Five months later, in October 2018, I got an email: "Dear Gregor, I spoke to Dorit, who runs the events at the Jewish Center in San Miguel, and she is excited at the prospect of bringing you down for a talk with your book! Would you be open to this? Claudia."

I Skyped with Dorit. We set March 3 as the date for an event we would call *Te Amo, Maria* (I love you, Maria).

Maria, Maria, Maria!

———◆———

Just as Claudia had so passionately painted me a picture back in Phoenix, when I arrived in San Miguel I discovered a place pulsing with colors and creativity. Folk art shops and museums littered the street corners, and there were some of the best art murals I'd seen since my stroll down Hosier Lane with Kiwi Carol in Melbourne. The city was chock full of charming town squares with native dancers and musicians, cobblestone streets, flat-roofed adobe houses, delicious street food, and welcoming locals. I'd read in a number of places that it was voted the #1 travel destination in the world. The downside of that is that American expats, especially as of late, had been reading the same literature—the place was teeming with them. But if you knew where to go, which I did because I had Claudia and Dorit, you avoided them as much as possible.

One of the city guides told me that the way the daylight hits the buildings and landscapes in San Miguel is similar to the way it hits them in the South of France, attracting the best artists and painters from all over the world. Claudia's boyfriend, Paul, who is Scottish, said he visited San Miguel for the first time a decade ago, fell big for it, and moved there permanently. He spoke of the city like it was a beautiful woman he lost his virginity to.

For my five-day trip, I stayed at the home of a local artist named Béa Aaronson, who was originally from France. The outside of her adobe brick building was classic Mexican stucco style, with a beautiful big red door, and an inside that could have been an abstract expressionist museum—as if Basquiat and Picasso got together one day and decided to fill a house with art. (I shot a *Humans in My Phone* at Béa's where you can see it all in person).

Most of the art was Béa's, who, like Ruth, is a prolific painter. Béa is also renowned in San Miguel for writing and performing staged readings based on the lives of some of her favorite artists. The venue she uses for those readings is where I'd soon be presenting *Te Amo, Maria.*

Béa was born in the wrong century—she belonged in old Parisian cafés sipping absinthe with her artistic contemporaries. I remember after Robin Williams died, Steven Spielberg said: "Robin was a lightning storm of comedic genius." For some reason, that quote always stuck with me. I feel like if Spielberg had met Béa, he would have substituted *comedic* for *artistic.* Like Robin Williams, the space between Béa's ears was a rushing river of salmon that never calmed. It was no wonder she needed so many different outlets for her restless ingenuity. We were fast companions.

She lived with a man named Jorge, whom she calls El Maestro. Jorge had lived in San Miguel for more than three decades. He was the kind of guy who couldn't take a walk without being stopped by someone he knew. He and Béa met at one of her weekly staged readings a couple years earlier. He went up to her afterward and asked her out on a date. A few weeks later, they moved in together. Jorge, now in his early eighties, is twenty-five years her senior.

At first handshake, Jorge was like the Mexican version of Clint Eastwood—the creased skin, the squinted eyes, the deep, resonant voice that spoke in slick, taut sentences, but as you began to feel his warmth and spar with his effortless humor, you wanted to adopt him as your Mexican uncle.

On the morning of my big presentation, Béa and I were eating breakfast at a café, waiting to be joined any minute by Jorge. I sat there scowling at my watch.

"Do you know anything about watches?" I asked Béa.

"Jorge does," she said. "He knows everything about watches."

Soon, Jorge joined the party. I showed him the watch.

"This watch I bought," I said to him, "do you see the face here? It's already bubbling underneath, water or something, I don't get it. I've never gotten it wet."

I pointed out the tiny bubbles forming under the surface.

"I'm just gonna return it," I lamented.

"Take the watch off," Jorge instructed sternly.

I unstrapped the band, handed him the watch, and he looked it over for a moment. Suddenly, a smirk grew on his face. What had The Maestro discovered?

He proceeded to *peel off plastic* from the face of the watch. It turns out that the bubbling under the face wasn't water; it was the protective cover that came with the watch. Once he peeled that off, the face was perfectly new and smooth.

"Holy shit!" I yelled out in shock. "You're a genius!"

Before joining in my jubilance, he flipped the watch over, examined the bottom, and looked up at me with a raised brow.

"Do you want me to take the plastic off the bottom too?"

I told that watch story in the introduction of my talk that evening, ending it with, "So, if you need your watch fixed, go to this man right here sitting in the front row." Jorge wasn't a big-crowd kind of guy, and I understood that, so I appreciated his agreeing to be there. The talk was for sixty people but it felt like it was for five. I was so grateful to Dorit for filling up every seat. Claudia, like Di in Australia, introduced me to the audience by sharing how we'd met around a pool in Phoenix. I got through the evening without crying. My friend Gregorij von Leitis, who had assailed my tears during all my other talks, would have no doubt been proud.

It was the first time I spoke about Maria publicly in a non-English-speaking country. One of my main drives has always been to spread Maria's love to all parts of the world, and never in my wildest imagination would I have thought one of those parts would be a little pueblo in Mexico. Maria continued to connect me with people helping me be the best possible version of myself.

On my final evening, Béa and I sat on her back terrace sipping scotch and smoking a joint, the latter of which I only do on special occasions. We finished the evening with the quintessential movie to watch while high—*2001: A Space Odyssey*. I had seen the film many times, but not for years, and it was the first time I watched it fully immersing myself in its genius. Maybe it was the Mexican weed, or maybe it was just that I was watching it exactly where I was supposed to be watching it.

CHAPTER 40

#VanLife

Part One

As I mentioned, I had eleven days of dead space starting July 21, 2019, before I could stay with Dana in Los Angeles. But I had bigger fish to fry before figuring that out—it was July 15, and there were two things happening in my world that needed my full attention: my subletter Paul was moving in, and my beatdown trial was set to begin, all in the same busy morning. I had to scoot Paul in quickly, hand over the keys, and make it downtown in time for the start of the trial.

Based on our phone conversations over the last few days, I imagined Paul as nothing other than a balding man of slight frame. But when I opened the door, there stood a thick-haired bodybuilder wearing a tank top and a caramel tan. He was an actor when he was in his twenties, which must have been thirty years ago, and staying at my Hell's Kitchen apartment was sentimental for him—during his theater days he lived just down the street.

Because I was in a rush to get to the courthouse, I handed Paul the keys and the Wi-Fi password, showed him my snake plant, and explained I wouldn't die if it happened to. I grabbed the roller bag I was set to live out of for the next forty-five days and headed downtown. After the first day of trial, I would take an Uber to my hotel in Chinatown and check in to begin my adventure. (I decided not to go to Brazil. The circumstance around that will arrive shortly.)

As I was walking to the subway to get to court, my phone rang: "Number Unlisted." *It must be the DA.* I answered it.

"Hi, Jamie, I'm just about to get on the subway."

"Don't get on. They plead guilty."

I screeched to a halt.

"So what does this mean?"

"It means the trial is not going to happen, and you have a free hotel for the week. Enjoy it."

It was behind me. It's not that the last few months had been especially traumatic for me; my head would heal, and the fits and starts of the trial dates never really affected my life. But one thought lingered: that I somehow attracted the incident. The beatdown itself wasn't my fault, but I knew I needed to calm down as I walked around the city. In Los Angeles, I had road rage; in New York, I have walk rage. And most of my walks are spent living in the future—*What am I going to eat tonight? Will I have time to go to the bank tomorrow morning? I have to remember to email Rebecca back.* I wasn't engaging in anything in front of me. I needed to use the beatdown as a way to take a deep breath and root myself in the moment.

Enter: attitude of gratitude. Gratitude that the shoulder-bumping posse didn't have any knives or guns that night, gratitude that Jamie had worked so hard in my corner for months at no cost to me, gratitude for Dana and Paul and his caramel tan, and gratitude for the hotel I never in a million years thought I would have. And it wasn't just a cheap room in a hostel, like I expected—it was a three-hundred-dollar-a-night luxury hotel. *When you open up your heart, good things happen.*

I used my time in the court-appointed hotel to dive into the manuscript I had abandoned after the summer with Nicole in the Hamptons the previous year. I also started watching the television series *Mindhunter.* Dean had been telling me for months how much I resembled Jonathan Groff, the lead actor in the series. I have to admit, it's like the guy stole my identity. In a way, feeling like I'm watching *me* helps me view myself with an objective eye, at least when the show is on.

Friday, July 20 came, and I spent my last night in the hotel. And where was I going to be for those eleven days before staying with Dana in LA? Looks like it was going to involve my friend Meng. But to fully appreciate Meng and what he had in store for me, you need to get to know him first.

Meng and I go back to 2006 to an acting school in Hollywood called Ivana Chubbuck Studios. We were both launching our acting careers at thirty years old. Neither of us had ever acted before, aside from, in my case, a sixth-grade production of *H.M.S. Pinafore* where I played Ralph Rackstraw. Our acting teacher at Chubbuck Studios, Darryl, assigned Meng and me as partners and gave us our first material to rehearse, a scene out of David Mamet's first play, *Sexual Perversity in Chicago*, which we would practice outside of class and then perform in class.

The Mamet scene involved two guys talking on a park bench, so Meng and I met a few times at the Jamba Juice on Melrose to rehearse on the outdoor patio, where we sat with our scripts in our chairs facing the street. We were often distracted by all the attractive women sauntering by in yoga pants. Meng was the worst. We could be completely immersed in our characters rehearsing our lines, and if a beautiful woman walked by, we'd have to start the scene over.

"Damn," Meng would say, shaking his head. "Did you see her? In the black yoga pants? Let's start over."

After we performed our scene in class, Darryl asked us how long we'd been acting. I was convinced we had bombed and was already thinking about what I was going to do after I quit the class—I knew I didn't want to return to the vapid world of reality television. In response to Darryl asking how long we'd been acting, I looked at my watch and responded, "About two minutes."

Darryl was taken aback, saying he figured we'd both been doing it for years.

Never in a million years would I have thought of myself as having acting talent. Because this was the first acting class I had ever taken,

Darryl's encouragement was the sole reason I decided to embark on an acting career. It was by and large derailed in 2008 when I was introduced to Maria—or more specifically, when I was introduced to my true self.

When the class ended a couple weeks later, Meng was given an opportunity to go to Berlin to work on a Steven Segal movie called *Half Past Dead*. He was hired as Segal's personal assistant as well as the stand-in/stunt double for Segal's costar, the rapper Ja Rule. After the movie wrapped, he decided to stay in Germany. We lost touch entirely.

Fast-forward to October 2014.

As you know, after Chuck died, I moved to New York and lived with Ruth. I had been at her apartment a couple weeks when one morning I was walking down Park Avenue to a bakery inside Grand Central Station that had the best chocolate croissant I ever tasted—the chocolate seeped out to the very edges of the bread (that almost never happens). As I headed down the east side of Park Avenue at about Fortieth Street, I looked up, and there he was ten feet away, ambling toward me with his head down.

After eight years, Meng and I just happened to be walking on the same sidewalk at the same spot three thousand miles away from where I saw him last. We jumped out of our shoes and embraced. He looked a little discombobulated. He had just flown into New York from Sweden, where he'd been living, and hadn't yet solidified a place to live. I told him I was living "right there"—I pointed out Ruth's building two blocks away. I said he could stay with me.

I had no reason to think Ruth would have a problem with a couple nights or so, but I decided not to tell her, thinking it would only cause tension. After she went to bed, I texted Meng, who was outside on the street waiting for me to come get him and bring him up. With Ruth asleep in the next room, Meng and I sat on my floor using our inside voices. He had known nothing of my quitting acting to become a caregiver in 2008, and I told him all about Maria and how strange and interesting it had been to live three lives in Los Angeles: my life as a reality television producer, my life as an actor, and my life as a caregiver. And here I was in New York living my life as a playwright. Meng ended up staying for two nights before booking a hostel. Without ever knowing, Ruth saved a man some stress.

In Sweden while living in a little town called Gothenburg, Meng had set acting aside and picked up photography, mainly fashion models. He showed me some of his work—all blonde Amazonian women posing in sprawling Swedish wheat fields. He loved telling me that you could walk into a 7-11 in Sweden and find beautiful models working there who had no idea they were beautiful. It was like old times, talking so passionately about women. I had to hand it to him—he had figured out a way to take one of his deepest passions, beautiful women, and get paid for it.

When we parted ways a few hours later, we vowed never to lose touch again. But we did for two years.

Spring 2016—*Ding!* A text arrived from Meng. It was a selfie of him on the street in front of an old vintage van from the eighties. He had just bought it for $1,500 and, to save some cash, was planning to live in it. A few weeks later, I got another text. It was a similar-looking van. This time he included pictures showing how he gutted the back and installed a queen-sized mattress covered in satin sheets and a comforter, redid the carpeting and curtains, and behind the driver's seat placed a little end table, on top of which rested a tiny potted plant, a box of chocolates, and an Evian water bottle.

Only this time he wasn't sleeping in it—he was renting it out on Airbnb.

The plan was to park the van in one of the nicest areas of Manhattan—West Village—where a hotel would cost two or three hundred dollars a night. Meng would charge seventy-nine dollars. Obviously, there was no running water in the van, but he had a gym membership from which he would acquire guest passes should the guest require them. Meng provided a charging brick in which guests could plug their phones or run a fan at night and a little push-button LED light for reading or finding things in the dark.

Over the next few weeks, Meng acquired four more vans that were occupied nearly every night on streets in West Village, mostly by twenty-and thirty-something European and Scandinavian couples eager to make their first trip to New York both affordable and memorable. Sometimes guests as close as New Jersey would book a van to have a place to crash after partying in the city. He bought a couple vans in San Diego and began Operation West Coast.

It didn't take long for New York media to discover Meng's vans, which were featured in things like *The Gothamist, Timeout Magazine*, and the *New York Post*. The headlines were to the effect of: "Can't afford a hotel in New York? Try one of these vintage vans!" The reporters had posed as guests in order to glean details for the article. Meng stayed in the shadows. He was less interested in being in the spotlight than building his five-star reviews and ensuring guests considered his version of the #vanlife 100% unique.

Aside from the "vanlife" hashtag starting around this time, copycats were inevitable. Many of the ads would feature identical-looking vintage vans and go as far as copying and pasting exactly what Meng wrote in his descriptions. Meng texted me a few screenshots of these ads, incensed people were stealing his idea. I looked at it as a compliment. He was the first to do it in New York, at least as far as I knew, and he was influencing others. And he did it *his* way—true success.

Meng had too many juicy stories to count. The most entertaining ones were the scariest or grossest, and he was such a great storyteller that you couldn't take your eyes off him. Every single word he spoke was filled with passion and vitality. One night he was dead asleep in one of his vans when the door swung open and a man jumped into the driver seat to steal the van. Meng, in his underwear, snapped awake and started screaming at the guy *"This is not your van!"* The guy had no idea he was storming into a van with an occupant in the back, so he jumped out of the van as fast as he jumped in. You can bet after that Meng made sure to remember to lock the van door at night.

Another time, at about six o'clock in the morning, he felt the van rocking back and forth, only to crack the curtain and see a shadowy figure leaning against the side getting a blowjob. Instead of confronting the duo, like I would probably have done, he decided to agonize through the rocking until they finished. He didn't park on that street anymore.

Meng loved to point out that the most difficult guests were almost always spoiled Americans complaining about every little thing. He preferred foreigners because they were more genuinely appreciative of the experience. Once, a Mexican couple flew in to New York for the first time, and because Meng always gave impeccable customer service, he offered to pick them up at the airport free of charge. On the way to the airport, Meng's van died. He had to call them and tell them to take an Uber. When the couple finally got to the van, tired, hungry, and with every right to be irritable, they didn't complain once. They were happy just to be there.

So Meng, I suppose in part because I'd let him crash at Ruth's when he first moved to New York, blocked out ten days for me to stay in one of his vans during the week before I was headed to LA to stay with Dana. It was going to be epic. I had keys to a van parked in beautiful West Village, a block away from the Hudson River. I could come and go as I pleased, and I could even decide to take a road trip if I wanted. All for zero dollars.

A heat wave hit New York that first weekend starting on July 20, 2019. As I lay in my van soaking in a pool of my own sweat, I texted Meng: "I'm getting a hotel room."

CHAPTER 41

#VanLife

Part Two

No. No way. I wasn't giving up this easily. I decided to stay put.

Here's what staying put looked like:

I'm sitting on the edge of the bed because I'm drenched in so much sweat that I don't want to lie down and get my sheets wet. I have no towel to wipe myself with. I can't stand up. I can barely even crouch. If I want to get dressed, I have to do it sitting down. If I want to pee—which I do in water bottles—I have to pee sitting down. I've never wished I were three feet tall until now.

My toiletries are all over the place and my LED light is too weak to find anything I need. I have one of those tiny clip-on fans plugged into the charging brick, but the brick is already down 20 percent and I've only had the fan going for ten minutes. I flip the fan off, instantaneously turning the van into a sauna. I can only have the fan on the lowest setting because if I turn it up to medium, let alone high, the battery juice dives twice as fast. I have to have the damn thing two inches from my face for it to have any cooling effect.

I'm naked and dripping wet. I'm sweating more naked than I am clothed. Doesn't that defy science? There is nothing to do in here but sweat. I can't concentrate on anything. It's too early to go to bed, but I'm too hot to expend energy putting on clothes to go outside where it's cooler ... and by cooler I mean 96 degrees. The van has windows but no breeze, so cracking them does nothing but make the trucks roaring by my window sound like they're driving through my skull. What am

I supposed to do in here? I pick up my phone and send Meng a text. "It's freaking boiling."

Meng texts back: "Van life, baby!"

He thinks it's funny? *He thinks it's funny.* I throw the phone down.

Somehow I get to sleep. I wake up in a cold sweat because my fan just sputtered out and died. The charging brick: zero percent. I'm in a sauna again. I look at my watch: It's four o'clock in the morning. *Fuck it.* I'm getting dressed and getting out of this furnace. I slip on some shorts and a shirt and exit the van into the dark of night. The whoosh of cooler hot air feels like heaven. I decide to take a stroll along the Hudson. The beauty of the glistening morning water gives me more energy. My walk turns into a jog, and I jog to Battery Park. Hello, Statue of Liberty. I return to the van. It's five o'clock in the morning. I grab the charging brick, my only hope for any sleep at night, and my laptop. I head to the Starbucks on Tenth and Hudson, plug the brick in, and start looking for a hotel. I ditch the hotel idea. I'm not giving up. If Meng can do it, I can do it.

The next night, much of the same: sitting, sweating, cursing, tossing, turning, leaving van, jogging to Battery Park, returning, grabbing brick and laptop, going to Starbucks, charging it, working on the book. Starbucks was always freezing. It was so cold I complained one day to the manager and requested the thermostat be turned down. Or up. Whatever "warmer" meant.

Later, Meng met me at the Starbucks, and I asked him if he was freezing. No, not in the least. I realized that spending two nights in a van exceeding 100 degrees had already affected my body temperature. Meng's body was used to it. We spoke about brushing teeth. I told him it was a hassle to have to use water in the van. Sometimes I'd be caught with only one water bottle—the bottle with drinking water—with no free bottle to spit the toothpaste into, or pee for that matter. Spitting the toothpaste out the window felt tacky. It was all too complicated.

"I don't use water, man," he said.

"You brush your teeth with no water?" I asked incredulously. I'd never thought of that.

Meng was teaching this "spoiled American" a lot about survival.

The heat wave left Monday, July 22, 2019, bringing me some much-needed Z's. I kept my daily routine and incorporated a new activity—an afternoon nap. It was the only way to get any restful sleep in.

One day a homeless guy in a wheelchair I'd seen rolling around my street stopped at my van. He had seen me go in and out and was curious about it. Meng always told me not to talk to strangers, to tell them I'm just traveling through. It's none of their business. I followed his orders.

"If only I had a van," the homeless guy dreamed out loud.

His name was Frank. He was in his fifties, had long curly brown hair, and was charismatic—he reminded me of Lieutenant Dan from the movie *Forrest Gump*. He had these red scabs all over his arms. They were rat bites. As he slept on the ground, they nipped at his flesh all night.

"Before bed every night," he explained, "I have to pour Clorox all over myself so they don't smell my flesh and don't know I'm there."

"Well, this van is boiling hot at night," I said in an attempt at making him feel better, "so at least you've got the fresh air."

After that interaction, I had regular flashes of Frank sleeping on the ground fending off rats. The images were hard to stomach. I imagined him sitting in his wheelchair, looking off into the Hudson, dreaming of owning a van. Then I imagined a wealthy person, sitting in his high-rise office, dreaming of owning an island. Then I imagined a monk sitting in his cave, dreaming of absolute nothingness. Everybody dreams about something.

Within a day the heat was history. It inspired me to clean up the van. Once I got everything in order, I felt like I just got a haircut. I had a new lease on life.

I wasn't taking showers, though. They were an inconvenience. The guest pass Meng gave me for the YMCA didn't work exactly as I'd imagine it would. I could only visit each location once. This worked for the typical guest usually only there for one or two nights, but because I was staying for eleven days, I needed to shower more than once. But if I wanted another shower, you see, I'd have to go to another YMCA location miles away. All my energy was being spent living in a van down by the river, not getting sleep, and somehow mustering enough energy to write at the ice cold Starbucks every day. I resolved that I was just going to have to stink to high heaven.

One morning I felt a bump on the back of the van and snapped awake screaming a bloodcurdling scream, expecting to see someone with a gun asking me where the keys were. Meng had me on edge after hearing that break-in story. It turned out a car behind me was trying to parallel park and had inadvertently tapped my bumper. I texted Meng, who was staying in a van about six cars down the street. "Did you just hear me scream?" I wrote. "Nah, what happened?" he wrote back. *Wait. Did I scream, or did I dream I screamed?*

At Starbucks one morning while charging my brick and working on the book, I took a break on an outside bench. A guy walking a miniature schnauzer sat down next to me. He noticed the Klimt tattoo on my right calf. He was an artist, and we talked about art for a while. People tend to open up around me, so he started telling me all about his physical problems and how he has to take medications every day.

"He's a lifesaver," he said, eyeing his dog. "When there's a certain scent in my breath, he licks my neck to remind me to take a certain medicine."

As we spoke, the dog made its way over to me, sitting comfortably at my feet. I started petting him.

"He doesn't do that with most people," his owner said. "He must feel comfortable with you."

I take on other people's emotions and energy very easily. I feel what others are feeling very quickly and intensely. Perhaps this makes me some form of an empath. So the fact that the script seemed to be flipped here, that this dog was taking on *my* energy, felt like a good thing. *Attitude of gratitude.* I was so grateful for Meng and for my van.

I ended up showering once in those eleven days. That one shower I got to take—at the YMCA on Bowery and Houston, next to the Whole Foods—was the best shower I ever took.

CHAPTER 42

The Will of Brazil

I had previously mentioned I'd tell you why I ended up nixing Brazil from my summer plans ...

Just after Dana's friend Paul—my trusty subletter—came into my life, I was planning my forty-five-day trip. I'd go to LA (Dana), then Brazil, then San Francisco (Christian), then Long Beach Island (Daniel), then Jersey City (Dean), and then home on September 1. Rio had been on the top of my list of cities to visit for years, but every time I would book a trip, my plane ticket always said "Europe." I had decided this year was going to be the year. I reached out to friends to see if anyone knew a Brazilian from whom I could glean travel tips. Brazil didn't exactly have the safest reputation, so I wanted to pick the brain of a native to get the real scoop.

It turns out Dean's wife, Manu, an actress from Italy, had a friend named Carolina who was Brazilian. Manu connected us. Carolina and I set a date to meet for a coffee at the Great Northern Café inside Grand Central Station. Four hours later we were still immersed in an ardent discussion about Rio and about life. Like the majority of Brazilians I had met, Carolina was a student of life, gregarious, and passionate about everything. And she didn't paint a glorified picture of her native city. Apparently her sister, who lives in Rio, had been robbed multiple times. Carolina even told me that I couldn't pull out my phone in public because *they*—the thieves hiding in the shadows—would take action at the first available opportunity.

"But it's okay, don't worry, you'll be safe, it's a beautiful city," she said, amused by the shock still on my face.

Carolina's sudden lightheartedness about her beautiful-dangerous country reminded me of Maria, who had a similar attitude about facing difficulties in beautiful-dangerous countries. Maria had a story about getting pickpocketed on a train in France. According to her, the French were the best pickpockets in the world.

"Well, at least they steal with a beautiful accent," is how Maria put a cap on it.

Because the café was closing soon, Carolina and I decided to finish up. I walked her to the 4-5-6 Subway inside Grand Central. We stopped at the entrance, smiled at each other and I leaned in to give a thank-you hug. I found myself headed for her lips—turns out she was on the same trajectory for mine. Suddenly, we were lip-locked, and the gates of passion flung open. This wasn't just a kiss; it was an attack-of-the-sexual-kind that neither of us saw coming.

We made out for about ten minutes in front of the crowds heading into the subway. If there were a bed nearby, we would have jumped into it. When the mouth intercourse stopped, we awkwardly giggled, and she disappeared down the escalator and into the subway chasms.

I didn't get much sleep that night. When I woke up the next day, something felt different. I no longer felt the pull of Rio, and I couldn't really figure out why. Part of it was hearing about the danger firsthand, but more of it seemed to be due to what had happened at the subway. I called Carolina to tell her I wasn't going to go because it didn't feel right for some reason. She felt guilty that she may have influenced my decision. I told her it wasn't really anything she said. Then it just tumbled out of my mouth.

"I felt like I already went to Brazil last night."

She laughed like it was some line from a movie, but it was the dead honest truth. That epic kiss had somehow erased—or replenished, depending on how you look at it—my passion to go to Brazil. It's a strange and magical insight, how when we follow our hearts we find that we don't *need* anything. It reminds me of two quotes, the first from Rumi: "We carry inside us the wonders we seek outside us." The second, from Deepak Chopra: "When you live from within, your desires are filled quickly, spontaneously, and with minimal effort." Of course we need outside things in our lives like people and vacations to feed us, but it's comforting to know that we really do have all we need inside us, and the more we understand that, the more outside things show up naturally.

But the main reason I'm writing this chapter, dear reader, is that the Brazil karma didn't end with Carolina. Oh no. Because you know what they say ... what you focus on, grows.

After I checked out of Hotel Meng, I flew to Los Angeles and stayed with Dana. I spent the week reuniting with old friends from the first of my three former lives in Los Angeles: reality television. One of the guys I reunited with—Shawn Antonio—I hadn't seen in eighteen years. On my first job in Los Angeles, I was a tape librarian for the television show *Blind Date*. Shawn was in casting. *Eighteen years later*, a couple months before my LA trip, I got a text from him out of the blue: "Gregor! What's up! It's been so long, just wanted to check in with you!"

His text happened to come in the middle of a string of dark days. We went back and forth a few times, the content of my texts becoming darker and more depressing. At one point, he said, "You know I'm a life coach now, right?" I didn't. I ended up booking a session with him that got me out of my head and back into the present. There is no way to explain that original accidental text he sent after eighteen years of silence, other than to say it was the universe knowing I needed it.

And then there was my friend Phil Brody, whom I hadn't seen in a couple years. We'd met in 2012 after we both wrote books and found each other through an author website. The day before I moved to New York in 2014, I saw him at a house party, and he said he had just taken up street art. He was experimenting with a typewriter stencil that would have an inspirational quote that he wrote written above it. Two years later, in 2016, I discovered an Instagram account with hundreds of thousands of followers around the world, called WRDSMTH—it was Phil! He had transformed himself into an internationally known street artist using that typewriter stencil. All my friends were doing well, and most importantly, they were pursuing their passions and doing what they loved.

Because I wasn't going to Brazil now, I had an extra week in Los Angeles with nowhere to stay. I had friends all over the city, but I didn't want to be the single guy intruding on married lives (which were the lives of pretty much every friend I have). So I booked a seedy hotel in Hollywood. I decided to go on the Bumble dating app to meet some girls. I connected with dozens that came and went, but one stuck. She lived in Venice Beach.

Can you guess what country she was from? You guessed it. *Brazil.* We agreed to meet at a bar called The Other Room on Abbot Kinney and hit it off both intellectually and physically. And she had a great sense of humor. I ended up staying at her place for the rest of my time in LA. On a side note, while in that bar with Anna, I noticed artwork I liked on the walls. I contacted the artist, Katya, and she ended up sketching the picture on the front of this book.

Now to round out the "everything comes in threes" Brazil motif, when I flew into San Francisco to visit Christian, he was still at work, so I took an Uber to his place from the airport. When I tell you this, you may not believe me, or maybe you will, if you believe in the rule of three. The driver was from …

Brazil! He was Brazilian!

Three Brazilians in one week—I had figured out a way to go to Brazil without ever setting foot in Brazil.

(Excuse me while I go grab some Brazil nuts.)

CHAPTER 43

Acceptance

"Make a wish! Make a wish!" yelled Christian, his wife, Suki, and my niece, Lyla.

I had no birthday wish in mind, but one just sort of appeared: to have full acceptance of my life. Whatever my life was, whatever it had turned into, I wanted to find a way to love it. For a guy who's spent much of his adult life wondering if he was living an incorrect life, acceptance seemed like a tall order. Regardless, whenever I was in San Francisco being an uncle, everything made sense.

I've been making it to San Fran to visit my brother, his wife, and their two kids about once a year, usually around the holidays with my mother. So when I arrived on August 14, we treated it like a bonus visit. Lyla was going to be turning seven the next day (and my birthday was a week after that, which we'd celebrate the night before I was set to return to New York), and my nephew, Sen, was eighteen months old. I'd last seen Sen a year ago when he was eight months old, and he was too young for us to bond. But this time Sen was running around the house playing the piano and climbing on the jungle gym down the street at Alamo Square Park. He even mumbled "Uncle Gregor" at one point—the first time he'd said it.

Whenever I set foot in the City by the Bay, every waking moment (and even some sleeping moments, as you'll soon see) are spent under Lyla's instruction. I am her yes-man. Suki, who is Korean, said to me, "Lyla is so lucky to have such a good uncle." Being a good uncle was biological for me. What human, presented with the gift of being an uncle, would ever want to show up late to work or not at all? I'm sure they exist somewhere, but not here.

Rounding out the family was Nuna, a ten-year-old white German shepherd who looked like what you would get if a giant mouse made love to Falkor the flying dog from the movie *The Neverending Story*. Nuna was the quintessential family dog. Aside from serving as a perfect fluffy pillow for anyone who needed one, her entire day was spent making sure the family stuck together. On walks, she would lag behind the group in case anyone went off course. In the house, if for example Sen went waddling into another room, Nuna was close behind to make sure he was safe. If dogs are a gift to humans, then Nuna feels like a gift to humanity.

I'm largely a private person outside of my books, but I loved being forced out of my comfort zone in San Francisco. Doors always remained ajar. Even at night, I had to leave my door open, because Nuna liked to come in and out multiple times to make sure I was okay. If the door was closed, she would have scratched at it all night thinking I may have been kidnapped.

If you're a critter of any kind, Christian and Suki's household is the one to be in. That first night before bed I noticed a spider on my wall—not a daddy longlegs or anything benign; it was a legitimately scary wolf-looking spider you only see in either horror movies or the Australia Outback. When I rather urgently warned Christian about it, he eagerly told Lyla to get the spider catcher. Assuming it was a mechanism to kill the spider, I was surprised to see Lyla scurry back with a long pole with a handle on one end and what looked like soft dish scrubber bristles on the other. She lined up the bristles to gently surround and enclose the spider without harming it. Once the spider was trapped, she ran to the front door, swung it open, and said, "Goodbye, spider!" as she released it onto Scott Street. Needless to say, I felt guilty about wanting to kill it.

Most mornings Lyla would get up before me, run into my room, jump onto my bed, and poke or tickle me until I gave her my full attention. The last time I visited, she was obsessed with stealing my comforter, making off with it before I even had a chance to fully wake up. This time, there was no comforter stealing, but she loved to startle me when I wasn't expecting it. If I dozed off with her in the room, which happened often on account of her being an indefatigable seven-year-old, watch out, because I was going to get a sudden *"Boo!"* through my eardrums. And for someone who dislikes loud noises— motorcycles and fire engines are the worst—it was something I needed to get used to.

One morning I was sleeping on my side, near the edge of my bed, and I opened my eyes to see Lyla, two inches from my face, watching me sleep. I screamed, "Ahhhh!" and she ran off, guffawing out of her skin. God only knows how long she was staring at me. That little stinker!

One day Lyla and I went to the San Francisco Zoo. She was mostly into the big cats: lions, tigers, and leopards. Our day consisted of chasing a wild peacock around a lunch table, taking a ride on the little train that choo-chooed through the zoo, and playing hide and seek on the playground. Still very much into what she calls *stuffies*—I'd always just called them stuffed animals—we couldn't leave without getting her one to add to her hundreds already at home. She wanted to get multiple stuffies, so I told her that her birthday gift only included one. With this new information, she took an extra amount of time to make sure she chose right. She finally settled on a red panda she named Reddy the Red Panda. She fell asleep hugging him on the Uber ride home.

When it was my turn to hug something on the way home—for my way home I was on an airplane to New York to stay with Dean in Jersey City before relieving caramel-tanned Paul of his subletting duties—I chose to hug a brother named Christian. It dawned on me over the last week in San Fran, and it's dawning on me as I write these words, that the Christian who always ran around life like it was a playground, who never overthought things, who never lost his cool, who befriended all the kids in school who had no friends—and who "never understood me and never would"—was someone I couldn't continue to pretend I didn't look up to.

One of the motivating factors in my writing the first book was to show that a woman like Maria actually existed—that she wasn't just a character out of novel. My decision to include my brother in this book, it turns out, is familiar territory: someone like Christian *actually exists*.

CHAPTER 44

FYH.

It's September 14, 2019, as I type these words. In about ten hours, I will turn this manuscript into my editor, Jessica, who edited my first book and who is another Earth angel Maria has introduced me to along this accidental journey.

Maria continues to introduce me to people. I was at a brunch last week at Christian Ebner's house—the Deputy Director of the Austrian Cultural Forum—and I met a ninety-two-year-old man named George Wolf, who, after telling him about my book, said he had met Maria once in the 1950s in New York and actually briefly worked for her brother-in-law Bernhard at one of his sweater factories. Needless to say, we had a lot to talk about.

Dear reader, you probably now know me better than most people in my life. Though I spend a fair share of time still living in fear, living life out loud in these books helps me keep the darkness at bay. My goal in life has not really been to acquire numbers or objects, it's been to acquire experiences and connection … and my success in achieving this goal has given me all the numbers and objects I need. A comforting thought came to me recently: if you follow your heart, Gregor, you will always be guided home. Home is a different place for everyone.

I was never fully honest with Maria. I never told her I loved her until the very end. And even then, I didn't say, "Maria, I love you." It was more, "You know I love you." It was a cop-out. I was scared. I loved her so much that I thought telling her would make it harder to cope once she was gone. And now that she's gone, I wish I told her more. But she knew. My actions always showed it.

Maria appears in my dreams every once in a while. She did at the end of summer shortly after relieving caramel-tanned Paul. I was in a building being paged. "Gregor, you're needed outside. Gregor, please report to the front of the building immediately … Gregor …" came the loudspeaker. On my sprint to the exit, people I sped by in the hallway were yelling, "Go, go, go! You can do it! She's waiting outside!" like I was running a marathon, and I was close, so close to the finish line. I finally made it outside, and there she was, standing erect and elegant, shooting out fireballs of euphoria from her eyes, waiting for me to run to her and hug her and tell her how much I missed her and hear how much she missed me. I woke up crying with so much joy and gratitude.

But, dear reader, I've had realizations while writing this book, even ones that are flowing as we speak. I'd like to put these thoughts in one final letter to Maria.

CHAPTER 45

Dear Maria

Maria Altmann
3065 Sky Boulevard, Apt. 7
Heaven Hills, Universe 90046

Gregor Collins
494 Ninth Avenue
New York, New York 10036

January 1, 2020

Dear Maria:

We're almost in 2020 and I feel just as bewildered by your impact on my life as I did in 2008 when I met you. I can only imagine after we parted ways in 2011 how surprised you must be at the lengths I've gone to introduce you to others. I'm sure I've unknowingly embarrassed you plenty of times, but I hope I've mostly made you proud. Often when I get really passionate about something, I end up eventually killing it. But you, Maria—you are unkillable.

I knew I wanted to write you a letter to close this sequel, just as I had done in the first book, and during most of the work, I was certain the letter would include all the standard endearments. But over the course of the last few weeks, and even as I write these words, epiphanies about our relationship continue to surface … one in particular has crystalized.

It's time for me to move on.

The passion it's taken me to keep this saga going, a saga no one but myself held me to, has depleted much of my energy. It's not by accident that in the nearly ten years I've been obsessed with you I've gone without a meaningful romantic relationship, not to mention a general lack of clarity about where I'm going. I said in the beginning of this book that when I write about you I'm the real me. Well I need to go work on being the real me *separate* from you. I think I've used you as a scapegoat to hide my fear of facing my life in an honest way.

You know how if the plane is going down they tell you to put our own mask on before you help someone else? This is me putting my own mask on now. It's taken me going through everything I needed to, to finally say, "Thank you for everything, Maria." And now it's time for me to be Gregor, and not "Maria Altmann's caregiver."

This isn't goodbye. You're in me, you always will be, and I'll continue to spread your love everywhere I go. But I'm moving out of the house. I don't live on Danalda Drive anymore. Where am I going now? I don't know. And maybe that's the beauty.

Just remember what you always told me: *Everything will be okay, My Love.*

Gregor

THANK YOU

Before I perform two short eulogies and give a few thank yous, I want you to know that I originally littered the middle of this book with photographs. Photographs were a big part of the journey in the first book, and I wasn't intending on changing that with this one - the problem was that the quality of many of them, especially in black and white, turned out poor. So instead of having some good ones and some bad ones, I decided to axe them all. I'm chagrined about it, but it gives me a chance to offer this: If you're curious about seeing any of them— they range from photos of Chuck, of Ruth, of the actual bison who wouldn't let me leave Yellowstone, even of the sketch that Ruth drew of me with the naked woman in the thought bubble—please email me at gregorcollins@gmail.com. It would be my pleasure to share them with you.

I want you to know about two special people who passed away during the writing of this book. First, Tommi Trudeau. Tom was Maria's original caregiver who one day in late 2007 called me and asked me if I ever thought about being one. The rest was history. Maria loved Tom dearly. Without him I never would have met her, but more importantly this world would have one less Sweetest Person in the World.

The second person is an actress named Libby Skala. We connected when I first moved to New York because we were both telling personal stories involving well-known Austrians—in her case, she would travel around the country doing one-woman shows called *Lilia!*, about her grandmother, Lilia Skala, who was an Academy Award-nominated actress from Austria. Libby was so smart and talented, and I was lucky enough to shoot her in an episode of *Humans in My Phone*. I send all my regards to her loving husband, Stephen.

Thank you to WIZO VIC (Melbourne), WIZO NSW (Sydney), and WIZO WA (Perth), who, upon my return to the Big Apple, led me to WIZO NY, WIZO Miami, and WIZO LA. To feel just a tiny part of an organization that has impacted the lives of Jewish women and children in Israel and around the world for more than a hundred years, is a true honor I'm not sure I deserve.

To president of WIZO NSW Diane Symonds, the author of the random Facebook message that fueled this book: like Maria, you've singlehandedly set my life in a new direction.

To all the wonderful ladies of WIZO Australia who opened up their homes and hearts to Maria and me: Paulette Cherney, Helen Granek, Dione Philips, Carol Rothschild, Hagit Ashual, Lorna Berger, Chavivah Van Der Plaat-Goldsteen, Shelley Seligmann, Ruth Kurc, Estelle Lin … just a few people whom I would, at the drop of a sombrero, drive to the airport for at three o'clock in the morning. Now four o'clock in the morning … That would be pushing it.

To Claudia Valentine, Susan Page, Dorit and Ari Arazi, Maestro Jorge, and the brilliant Béa Aaronson: thank you for making my stay in San Miguel de Allende unforgettable. We shall meet again.

To my close friends and family, who despite what masks I put on, persist in seeing the real me: Without you, I would disappear completely.

To you, dear reader: Thanks for memories. I'll see you again.

GC

Printed in the United States
By Bookmasters

Printed in the United States
By Bookmasters